FIRST A BEAR: NOW A SAINT

MIKE DITKA'S INSIGHTS, OUTBURSTS, KUDOS, AND COMEBACKS

Jim Stamborski

Lifetime Books, Inc.

FH JH

Library of Congress Cataloging-in-Publication Data
Ditka, Mike.
    First a Bear, now a Saint : Mike Ditka's insights, outbursts, kudos & comebacks / [compiled]
by Jim Stamborski.
        p. cm.
    ISBN 0-8119-0872-0 (pbk.)
    1. Ditka, Mike--Quotations. 2. Football coaches--United States--Quotations.
    3. Football--United States--Quotations, maxims, etc. I. Stamborski, Jim, 1947- II. Title.
    GV959.D58 1998
    796.332'0973--dc21   98-18580
                                                                                 CIP

Cover photo courtesy of AP/Wide World Photos
Interior Design by Vicki Heil
10 9 8 7 6 5 4 3 2 1
Printed in Canada

TABLE OF CONTENTS

Preface _____ v

Introduction _____ ix

1. Ditka On Ditka _____ 1

2. Witty Mike _____ 7

3. The Psychological Aspects of Pro Football _____ 15

4. The Physical Aspects of Pro Football _____ 27

5. The New Bears Coach _____ 35

6. The Bears Organization _____ 39

7. Buddy Ryan and Mike Ditka _____ 51

8. McMahon, Perry and Payton _____ 57

9. Player Interaction 1982-1992 _____ 71

10. Chicago and the Grabowskis _____ 81

11. The Hated Packers _____ 85

12. Ditka From Those Who Know Him _____ 89

13. Ditka and the Media _____ 97

14. Winning and Losing: 1982-1985 _____ 105

15. Losing the Edge: 1986-1987 _____ 115

16. The 1988 Season: Injuries and a Heart Attack _____ 127

17. Overcoming a Lack of Talent _____ 131

18. Fired! _____ 147

19. New Saints Coach _____ 153

20. Getting the Saints Ready _____ 159

21. Current Saints Offensive Players _____ 171

22. Current Saints Defensive Players _____ 183

23. The 1997 Season _____ 191

A Note To Our Readers:
Unless otherwise indicated, all quotes are those of
Mike Ditka as taken from the *Chicago Tribune*.

PREFACE

From 1988-1992 the Bears never reached the same premier team status they reached in 1985-1987. In January of 1993 the Bears let Mike Ditka go. The question New Orleans Saint fans now ask is what happened to the Super Bowl dominating Bears after the 1985 season?

Several factors contributed to the decline of the Super Bowl Bears, who at the time were the youngest team ever to win the Super Bowl. Most of these factors were outside the control of Mike Ditka.

Upon the death of George Halas in November of 1983, Mike McCaskey became the president of the Chicago Bears. It was said at the time that although Mike McCaskey was George Halas' grandson, he was unprepared to run the Bears. An Ivy league graduate, McCaskey was in many ways the antithesis of the personalities of Ditka and Halas.

Halas and Ditka were the Bears, tough and hardscrabble. McCaskey became the Bears' president by the good-fortune of his birthright. Whereas McCaskey seemed more comfortable crunching numbers in a pin-striped suit in a high-rise Fortune five hundred board room; Ditka and Halas were more comfortable crunching heads on the football field. To the fans, McCaskey looked uncomfortable in the presence of Mike Ditka and mingling with Chicago's football fans. Ditka, on the other hand, always said he could drink a shot and a beer in any Chicago tavern and be just one of the guys. Reportedly, McCaskey wouldn't allow beer in his Soldier Field skybox.

The first inkling I had that all was not right in Beardom was when Jim McMahon arranged to have an acupuncturist treat his injured hip in New Orleans just before the Super Bowl. In McMahon's words:

> *McCaskey doesn't have to worry about controlling the club. And I don't care who pays for the doctor. Main thing is he's here. Mike Ditka was all for it. So was Jerry Vainisi. I don't know why McCaskey got so uptight.*

This was one of the earliest indications that Jim McMahon did not think much of the Bear owner. In the two years after the Super Bowl McMahon became increasing vocal and public in his criticism of Mike McCaskey.

Super Bowl fever in 1985 featured loud and lusty barking by fans approving of the Bears junk-yard dog defense. According to members of Chicago's media, when McCaskey tried barking he sounded like a poodle. After the Super Bowl there seemed to be a struggle behind closed doors in the Bear organization between Mike Ditka and Mike McCaskey. At this time, Mike Ditka's popularity in Chicago was such that he probably could have run for mayor of the city of Chicago and won easily. Ditka got all of the press and all of the glory, while Mike McCaskey received very little. George Halas had a reputation as being tight with a dollar when it came to salaries, a tradition carried on by McCaskey. After winning the Super Bowl in January of 1986, the first major loss was Wilbur Marshall going to the Washington Redskins for $6 million.

The next year, unfortunately for the Bears, McMahon sat out the 1996 preseason because of injury. Shortly after coming back for the regular season, McMahon was injured again and was out for the season. McMahon's injury-plagued season became the next factor in the decline of the Chicago Bears; it marked the signing of Doug Flutie. The perception of some of the Bear players, notably Jim McMahon, was that the Bears already had good depth at the quarterback position with Mike Tomczak, and Steve Fuller.

Publicly it seemed that Ditka was convinced that Flutie could win in the NFL in a big way. To the Bear players it must have seemed that the coach was tampering with the chemistry of the team and threatening the position of Jim McMahon, the heart and soul of the team, or that McCaskey was attempting to squeeze out McMahon because he was becoming increasingly critical of Bear management.

The next crisis that rocked the Bear organization was in January of 1987 when Jerry Vainisi, the Bears general manager and Ditka's best friend, was fired. This move by McCaskey, which was never fully explained, cut Ditka to the bone. In his tearful words to the Chicago media, Ditka explained:

Let me just say that I was totally taken by surprise, totally. And I was very, very hurt. Jerry Vainisi is respected in our business as one of the best. And he deserves that because he's earned that. It was his (Halas') last wish that Jerry be the general manager and that I be the coach or it would have been changed....You just don't cut an appendage from your body and then go on and live normally. As I say, Jerry Vainisi's a class person and he'll end up in good shape. I really don't have anything to say.

Ditka also noted:

I learned as a kid the guy who owns the ball and bat can call the game any time he wants to. So I accept that.

Here in public it was Ditka's way of saying that the Bears executive took his bat and went home because he didn't like the way the game was being played.

The next major problem was more of Ditka's doing and that was his reaction to the 1987 football players strike. Ditka's striking players felt he was out of line pretending that the non-striking "Spare Bears" were NFL caliber players. After the strike, Ditka asked for a vote from the previously striking Bear players to accept the "Spare Bears" on the roster. Reportedly, the vote was 44-1 against the non-union Bears and Ditka promptly vetoed the vote explaining:

I let them vote because I thought they'd be realistic about it. If someone could help our team, I thought they'd let them. But they saw fit not to do that. The only thing I worry about is winning games. I'm not in a popularity contest. A lot of those guys made a lot of decisions the past four weeks. I'm the boss now. I make the decisions and live with them.

And later in 1988:

I didn't feel close to the players at all [in 1987], and they didn't feel close to me. I totally disagree with what the American athlete is doing. Football is good for everybody. When you've got to rape the game, you've got a problem. Everybody talked about how they felt betrayed. I felt betrayed, too. I shouldn't be saying this now, but something should be said. Whether I'm close or not, it's important to have a great amount of respect, and maybe that's what wasn't there on either side.

From 1989 to 1992, poor football personnel decisions by the Bear organization and injuries to key players, resulted in mediocre teams. Yet, Ditka, by the strength of his football knowledge and motivation skills, kept the Bears competitive. Even so, after a 6-10 season in 1989, the Bears rebounded to 10-6 and 11-5 seasons in 1990 and 1991. Finally, after a 5-11 season in 1992, Ditka waited to see if Mike McCaskey wanted him back as coach in 1993. McCaskey didn't and fired Mike Ditka in January of 1993.

Even then, true Mike Ditka fans knew he would be back in coaching and as Ditka said upon being named coach of the Saints: *This time we're going to do it right.*

For those of you who think that Mike Ditka will have trouble becoming a New Orleans Saint, the transition had been made; and Coach Ditka is not looking back. Believe him when he says: "I'm a Saint. Nothing else. I'm a Saint through and through." Believe it, sit back Saint fans and enjoy the ride. It's going to be a great one.

INTRODUCTION

In the words of Mike Ditka:

I'm a big guy about quotes, because I believe in them. A pretty good coach one time, Vince Lombardi, made this statement. He said the difference between success and failure in people is not a lack of strength and not a lack of knowledge. But, basically, it's a lack of will. There will be no lack of will in this organization. And anybody who has a lack of will, will not be here. New Orleans Times-Picayune *1/29/97*

I am Mike Ditka's biggest fan. From 1982-1992 I collected Coach Ditka's quotes from Chicago newspapers, and again in 1997 from the New Orleans newspapers. I did this because Mike Ditka reminds me of family and friends who are tough, hard-working decent people just like Ditka and his family and friends in the steel mill town of Aliquippa, Pennsylvania. Looking back over the years, I realized what a rare and special commodity Mike Ditka is in professional sports, and how his quotes about football and his life's philosophy have been important to me. His philosophy has been an inspiration to me in my work and in my family life. This book is, in reality, a historical document representing the history of Mike Ditka's coaching career in New Orleans and his years as a head coach for the Chicago Bears.

I was fortunate to talk to Mike Ditka in South Florida at the Miami Baptist Hospital's dedication of an intensive care unit for heart attack patients. At that time, I asked him if he would ever consider coaching the Miami Dolphins. He was very diplomatic and responded that Don Shula could coach the Dolphins as long as he wanted to, but if he ever did retire, he would consider coaching again if there was an offer on the table. I knew then that Coach Ditka would be back coaching somewhere soon.

Saint fans are lucky. Although they may not realize it now, they will soon realize that Mike Ditka is a great coach. If he had a supportive owner in Chicago, the Bears would have easily won several Super Bowls in the late 1980s and early 90s. To several members of the media and others in the Bear organization, Bear owner Mike McCaskey seemed to undermine Mike Ditka's position as the Bear's head coach. Ditka was always in Chicago's spotlight, receiving adulation and praise, while McCaskey was relegated to competing for the spotlight. Chicagoans knew that McCaskey inherited his position as owner of the Bears and in a city of Grabowski's, defined as hard-working tough blue collar workers, McCaskey was perceived as the lucky rich kid.

In 1997, many thought Ditka, as the New Orleans Saints head coach would be a kinder, gentler coach. I think Ditka believed that he would be as well. Yet, having followed coach Ditka for more than a decade, and knowing his intensity, I wondered what would be the match igniting the explosion. It didn't take long. Those watching the Saints third game of the season against the 49ers, remember seeing Saints quarterback Heath Shuler miss a wide open Saints receiver in the end zone shortly before the end of the first half. On the sidelines, although Ditka seemed to be controlling himself, I thought he was about to lose it. And, I found out later he did lose it in the lockeroom at half-time. To my relief, the real Mike Ditka was back.

Mike Ditka's intense winning attitude will be infused in his players. If they don't perform, they will be gone.

I'm sure Ditka felt that he had a chance with the Bears, after the Super Bowl victory in January of 1986, to win many more Super Bowls. Everything was in place to give coach Ditka a chance to be known as the greatest football coach of all time. Bad luck, a jealous owner, and his own intensity prevented it from becoming a reality.

The New Orleans Saints will be the vehicle for Mike Ditka to receive the proper credit for being one of the greatest football coaches of all time. Write this down Saint fans: you will have your team in the Super Bowl in four years or less. More than anything else, Mike Ditka needs to have an owner who sits back and lets him do his thing. Tom Benson seems to be that type of owner. The first indication that Mike Ditka was interested in the Saints came in October of 1997 when he told a Chicago paper:

[Benson] has been a good owner because he hasn't got real involved. He's hired people and let them do their jobs. They need someone who will help fill that stadium...winning will do that. If an offer came up I'm not sure what I would do. I'm 99 percent sure I'm not interested, but sometimes that one percent can be a powerful thing. New Orleans Times-Picayune *1/26/97*

Many people have asked me why Mike Ditka would go back to the high-pressure world of coaching in the NFL since he is a multi-millionaire who could spend the rest of his life perfecting his golf game. Coach Ditka answers this question the best:

Life for me is about challenges and climbing mountains, and that's what I intend to do, try to climb another mountain. Our goal in the Saints organization will be to be the best we can be, to maximize our total potential in every area by every player, by every person in this organization, by every coach, by every person in management. I want to create a sense of pride, a greater sense of pride in what this organization is all about. Some people say why, and I say why not? It's not going to come easy, but nothing good in life ever does come easy. It's going to be fun doing that.
New Orleans Times-Picayune *1/29/97*

New Orleans Saints players wondered what to expect from Coach Ditka. He probably said exactly the same thing to them that he told the terrible Chicago Bears players in his first year of coaching. Dan

Jiggetts was in the room in 1982 when Ditka addressed his Bear players:

> *He came in with a clear vision and said, 'We are going to the Super Bowl and we're going to win it and anybody that doesn't believe it can hit the door.' That was the kind of thing we wanted to hear. And a few years later, that's what happened."*
> New Orleans Times-Picayune *1/30/97*

Another native son of Ditka's home town of Aliquippa, Pennsylvania, Tony Dorsett explains:

> *He's a no-nonsense type of guy. Today's athlete, that's what you need. What's hurting Dallas now, and there's nothing wrong with being a player's coach—but I think guys have got to have that respect and fear factor, like they had under Jimmy [Johnson, former Dallas head coach]. He had the attitude, 'If you don't do your job, I'll find somebody to do it for you.' That's the kind of coach Ditka is. This franchise [the New Orleans Saints] looks like it can use that.* New Orleans Times-Picayune *1/30/97*

What else can Saint players expect? As in the past, Ditka will expect his Saints to be well-conditioned:

> *If they couldn't pass the conditioning test last year, they'll die this year. New Orleans Times-Picayune 1/31/97*

On winning:

> *Our goal is to win. It's not win later. It's to win now. I don't believe in living in the past. I believe the past is for cowards. You live in the past, you die in the past. The past has nothing to do with what this organization is doing from this day forward."*
> New Orleans Times-Picayune *1/29/97*

For the first few years Saint fans can expect the team to follow Ditka's start up plan:

We're going to try to be a very no-nonsense type of football team. We're going to try to exert as much pressure as we can defensively on our opponent. And we're going to try to put as much pressure as we can on the opponent's quarterback as we can with our defense. We intend to be a multiple-front defense and a multiple-coverage defense. On offense, I wish I could tell you I was a genius. But I'm not a genius, and I never professed to be a genius. You will see us run the football. You may not like that. You may think that's boring. But I did that for a long time in Chicago, and it worked. We're going to learn to run the football before we can learn to pass it. Once we learn to run it, we'll see if we can figure out how to pass it.
New Orleans Times-Picayune *1/28/97*

Finally, coach Ditka is a bear no more, working on sainthood in New Orleans. But for those of you who think Mike Ditka has mellowed a little over the years, he has a final word for you:

I have softened, but don't push me.
New Orleans Times-Picayune *2/2/97*

Coach Ditka, May You Live 100 Years !!!

DITKA ON DITKA

Mike Ditka, Competitor

I hate to lose. When I was a kid playing Little League baseball, boy I hated to lose. I cried. It just hurt my feelings to lose. I don't like to lose. I'm not proud of that, but I just don't like to lose. 11/17/85

I wasn't a guy who went up and shook hands before the game or after the game. 12/13/85

I'm a loner to a degree. I did a lot of things on my own. Why should I let what anybody else thinks affect me? I think I know much more about what I'm doing. I'm always going to get criticized. When you have success and set a standard, expectations are so high, you can't always reach them. We live in a society that hates to see people be successful. If someone is doing well, they try to drag him back down. I can't be a hero or friend to everybody. We're only here for a few moments. How many people can you touch? So you've got to do it your way. 11/13/89

I'm not a guy who sets a goal and then changes it the next day. I might change it up, but I won't change it down. 8/30/88

My intentions are good, but sometimes my methods stink. 11/14/89

Dave Michiels, team psychologist for the Saints, replied, after being asked by a reporter what motivates Mike Ditka:
He hates to lose. He despises losing, and I'll tell you why. It's not because of him. I don't know if anybody will ever understand this. It's because he feels he let the team down. He takes so much on his shoulders and feels so responsible for these young men and winning. I have never met anyone in my life more team-oriented than Mike Ditka. 10/10/97 *New Orleans Times-Picayune*

RIGHT AND WRONG

If I got a whipping in school, I'd come home and get another one from my dad. He didn't go to school to find out why. He assumed I was wrong, and that's how it should be. Today we live in a different society. We entrust our teachers with our children's education, but won't allow them to discipline them. That's a bunch of crap. 11/13/89

Mike's brother, Ashton Ditka:
We come from openness. When we grew up there was no reason to BS around. You said what you thought. He's still the same. 11/13/89

Mike Ditka, Player

Pain never bothered me. 8/24/97 New Orleans Times-Picayune

On his years at Pittsburgh University:
I also hit the bottom in Philadelphia, just a bust-out player with a bad hip and knee and foot, ready to quit until I came to Dallas. 1/24/82

I was told I'd be a backup [at Dallas] and that hurt. And that's what I was, because I didn't do all I could that first year. But the next year I started. I worked harder than anyone else in the off-season. Nobody ever worked harder. I ran in my bare feet to toughen my bad foot. I did everything I could, especially weights and running. I got in such good shape, I could have done anything a 21 year old kid could do, and I was 30. I dropped my weight 21 pounds until everything was muscle. And I caught more passes the next year than any tight end in Dallas history. 1/24/82

I think that's where I understood that the harder you work, the more you get of life. I became a pretty good football player, not because I was faster or could catch the ball better, but I taught myself to do a lot of things that other guys didn't. Everything was competitive. My whole life was based on beating the other guy, doing better, being equal to, or just showing I could be as good as anybody else. I don't know if that's good or bad. 11/17/85

Most of the guys played with pain because they were afraid to come off the field for fear someone would take their job.
8/24/97 New Orleans Times-Picayune

I'm not saying it's right or wrong. Maybe what Alex Karras said in that movie, *Against All Odds*, is right. Maybe we were all dumb for doing it that way. But the only security you had back then was playing and playing well. If you weren't playing, it meant somebody else was playing, and your security blanket was taken away.
8/24/97 New Orleans Times-Picayune

After a dislocated foot injury during his playing career:
I started favoring it and getting pulled muscles. My back started hurting. Eventually, my hip started hurting. [The foot injury] didn't heal fast enough to get me back on the field. It healed crooked. That's life. I can't help it. Now guys say, "I was released from the team when I pulled a hamstring." Well, tough. So what?
8/24/97 New Orleans Times-Picayune

DESTINED TO BE A BEAR

My personality is the Bear's personality, and I saw it when [Dallas] played them [the Bears] this year. I saw things that rekindled that old feeling, that old look. The toughness. They really came after us. I really liked what I saw. I didn't like the bad execution in certain areas, but I did like the physical end of it. 1/24/82

Don't get me wrong. I'm a realist. I understand what the situation there is. I understand it's not gonna be the fair-haired son coming home and everything is gonna be beautiful and the sun is going to rise and set on the city of Chicago and the Bears. That's not what I'm saying. I'm saying the opportunity is going to be there and that's where I want to be, that it's been a life-time ambition to be there. 1/24/82

It's the only thing I've ever wanted to do in my life. I'm very happy, and I welcome the opportunity and challenge for three more years. It started when Mr. Halas made the decision and I thank God he made it. I'm sure a lot of people doubted the decision. 1/3/85

Mike Ditka, Coach

I wish I could say I'm not going to get excited anymore but that's not my nature. I don't apologize. I wish I could stand out there like [Bud] Grant or [Tom] Landry but I can't do it. 9/27/83

My biggest problem is myself. I think I take coaching too seriously. It's my job. But more than that, it's pride. The main thing to remember is, when you let your guard down, don't get thrown off the track. Just remember what's at the end. 7/14/85

Could Ditka the player have played for Ditka the coach?
Yeah. Because I want to win. That's the only thing I want to do. If a player wants to win, he should have no problem. If he wants to be

patted on the butt every time he does something wrong, then he'll have a problem. 10/30/85

There's no question that when I stand up and talk, a lot of guys say, "Here we go again." 11/17/85

You live in life on gut instincts. I've lived on gut instincts my whole life. I've made a lot of them that are wrong and I've made a lot that have been right. 10/30/89

I'm the first person who says my way may not be the right way, but it's my way. I'm entitled to it. For all these analysts and all these jerks who gripe and complain, I'll put my record up against some of these other yokels who do it their way. Doesn't make me right, but it makes it my way. That's why we're individuals in life. You're not supposed to be a clone of somebody else. 10/29/89

DITKA ON HIS PLAYERS

I'm not a tough guy. My God there's not a coach in the league who bends over backward to congratulate, to build up his people more than I do. But when they're wrong, they're wrong. 11/1/83

They play hard because I think they know they have to play hard to stay on the field. There's nobody I wouldn't replace. 11/17/85

Sometimes players feel I don't think they're important to the team. That's not true. 7/17/86

DITKA, JUST AN ORDINARY GUY

I can walk up to any steelworker or any garbage collector in the country and I can sit down and talk life with them. I don't care if I've got a pair of Gucci shoes on or I've got a pair of clodhoppers on. 12/28/86

1988: Hall of Fame

On February 2, 1988, Mike Ditka was officially voted into the professional football Hall of Fame:
It's not an individual honor. I had coaches. I had teammates. I had a quarterback who threw me the ball. I had a coach who designed an offense that threw the ball to the tight end and changed the look of pro football in the early '60's. It's really nothing I did. I just played the position as good as I could, the way Mr. Halas designed it. 2/3/88 Chicago Sun-Times

What the Hall of Fame means:
It means people are going to recognize you in the same breath with Sid Luckman and George Halas and Bronko Nagurski. When you start thinking about all those names, you say, "Hey, this is awfully special." I've been able to do things I once only dreamed about. When I look back and think about all the fun I had playing, to have an honor like this bestowed upon me is mindboggling.
2/3/88 *Chicago Sun-Times*

I don't think anything I did was great. If I'm going to be remembered for anything, I played hard. I gave it the best I could. I think the people who played me would vouch for that. I never asked for anything and I never gave anything. I wasn't a friendly guy. I wasn't a hand-shaker, but I wasn't meant to be. I was trying to beat the other guy. Hand-shaking and butt-patting are things that came in lately.
2/3/88 Chicago Sun-Times

I really don't have a private life anymore. I guarantee I signed more autographs in two days [at the Hall of Fame] than these players signed all week. It's important to take the time to do it, but after a while it becomes hard to do constantly. 2/8/88

Early Signs of a Sense of Humor

During Ditka's career as a Bear player a fan ran onto the field during a Bear-Ram game. Ditka flattened him. In one of his first press conferences with the Chicago media Ditka said:
Well, I'll tell you this, if a fan ran onto your desk, where you work, what would you do? 1/21/82

What Ditka calls Dick Butkus:
Mr. Butkus. I always called him Mr. Butkus and if any of you get as mean as Mr. Butkus I'll call you Mr., too. 2/10/82

Ditka's philosophy on two minute drills:
Score. What do you think? Give up. 11/8/83

Ditka's Hometown

How tough was Aliquippa?
Our definition of quick hands was a guy who could steal hubcaps off a car that was moving. 6/15/87

7

There was a guy named Pete Maravich, who led the NBA in scoring. Then there was a guy who didn't play sports, but he made some pretty good music. Henry Mancini. Actually, Henry's from West Aliquippa but after he got famous we moved him into town. 6/15/87

Of course, the most famous football player from Aliquippa is a guy named Tony Dorsett. Ditka, Dorsett. A lot of people liked to compare us. I can understand that. I thought about it a long time. You look at it this way: both of our names started with 'D.' Before I changed barbers, we both had curly hair. We're both Ukrainian. See, Tony's real name was Dorsett-ski. We both attended the University of Pittsburgh. And we've both worked for the Cowboys. I've analyzed this over the years, and let me tell you the differences between Ditka and Dorsett. It's simply 17 years and a million-and-a-half dollars. You figure out who's got which. 6/15/87

It's silly to keep a camera on a coach, especially this coach. Lots of coaches put people to sleep. Put it on me and guys want to go out and buy a gun. 12/17/86

DITKA'S PERSONALITY

We're not going to talk about my personality because I have none. 10/30/86

Johnny Carson: *Didn't the players call you Sybil because of your change of personalities?*
Ditka: *That wasn't the reason. I changed dresses three times a day. 1/21/87* Chicago Sun Times

There's only two; Jekyll and Hyde. There is no third personality. 12/28/86

I'm a flake. Just write that. I'm a flake. I got a lot of split personality and stuff like that. If you're in the right place at the right time, you'll probably see me in a dress. 12/9/97 Miami Herald

IT WASN'T EASY COACHING THE BEARS

**After a streaker ran onto the field during the
Cowboys-Bear exhibition game in London:**
I had to look around and see if it was anybody from our bench.
8/4/86

Thinking ahead to playoff games?
*Not me. I'm just a poor Polack. I can't look much past next Sunday
in Detroit.*

**Back tracking on the reasons why he selected
Kevin Butler over Bob Thomas:**
I lied. 9/3/85

*I can tell the players are getting ready when they gripe and complain
and get mad at me. I heard it today a little. So we're coming on and
making some progress. 8/5/86*

I said to the team, "I'd like you to meet Doug Flutie," and a couple
of the guys threw tomatoes at me, but that's all. I think I heard them
saying to him after practice, "Let's have a 7-up." 10/23/86

On Bear veterans being late to training camp:
*I heard five or six guys missed a plane from O'Hare to Dubuque.
That's all right. They all have money. They're all multimillionaires.
They know how to rent a car. Some probably know how to hot-wire a
car. 7/16/86*

**On the match up between the 49ers offense, directed
by Bill Walsh, and the Bear defense, directed by Buddy Ryan:**
They're going to put up two signs, "Geniuses at work." 1/6/85

*I don't like late games, I hate them. You're supposed wake up, go to
church, eat breakfast, go play football—at noon. Then you're
supposed to go home and eat dinner.* When told some of his players

preferred night games: *Do they? Who said that? Jay Hilgenberg? Well, he doesn't get out of bed until two, that's why. 10/16/90*

Is the pressure of the Bears-Giants game getting to you?
I-I-I-I'm not used to being in this spot. I'm the one getting nervous. I think [the team] is OK. They've been through too many big games to let it bother them too much. My attitude is what's bothering me. 9/12/87 *Chicago Sun Times*

Ditka described the Bear-Giant game as having global significance. After defeating the Giants, Ditka was asked to describe the next game against Tampa Bay:
That was global. This is galaxy. 9/16/87

After the 31-29 loss to the Broncos, Ditka was told that some of the Bear players would be singing for charity that week:
I'm surprised they don't do it at 11 a.m. Sunday and tie it in with the warmups. 11/18/87

Did the players put Ditka in their doghouse as a result of his veto concerning non-union Bears?
My dogs are in the kennel and they're not even mad at me. Take a look at this guy—how can you be mad? 10/23/87 Chicago Sun Times

Referring to Bear rookie Joe Johnson as Joe Jackson:
He's not 'Shoeless Joe' but he could be 'Pants-less Joe' if he gets beat a few times. 8/9/91

On Bear punt returner Johnny Bailey's mishandling of punts:
We've got a dungeon downstairs. We'll take him downstairs and flog him. 9/10/91

DITKA ON WILLIAM PERRY

I don't think we will ever regret this pick. He can have the impact of a Big Daddy Lipscomb. He's going to look good in that navy blue uniform, or two uniforms, whatever it takes. 5/1/85

Why Ditka picked Perry in the draft:
Gut feeling. 5/1/85

I once played against a guy who weighed 415 pounds. We ate his lunch. 5/1/85

On Raider defensive end Howie Long's criticism of Perry:
I never argue with anybody as smart as Howie Long. Or is it Huey Long? 11/8/85

We want [Perry] around 300 [pounds] but we don't know what he'll be. He worked out religiously until a week ago and then he went home to South Carolina. That's usually a catastrophe. The chicken population of South Carolina goes down measurably. 7/16/86

He's running twice a day. From the refrigerator to the bathroom. 7/21/87

DITKA ON JIM MCMAHON

I've never spoken behind sunglasses before, but now I understand why Jim does it. He likes to escape reality. 4/28/87

Why McMahon & Brian Bosworth can't be on the same team:
There wouldn't be enough sunglasses to go around. 4/15/87

Does it bother him when Jim McMahon talks about him?
Doesn't bother me. I kinda like Jim. He makes me laugh and I don't laugh that much. 11/14/86

On McMahon's mohawk haircut:
I think it's very nice. I can relate to that. He did it on his own and I tried to do that once in a training camp. Ended up like his Mohawk all over. You can't correct those things once you make the wrong slice. 7/26/85

This is my sixth year with the Bears. Jim McMahon has been with the Bears six years, too, and people say we don't communicate. That's not true. We've talked four times. 6/15/87

Everybody asks me, "What kind of a relationship do you have with Jim McMahon?" I say it's strange and wonderful. He's strange and I'm wonderful. 6/15/87

What McMahon is doing to rehabilitate his shoulder:
He's hitting the 5-iron about 180 yards. 4/24/87

I'm going to tell you one story, and Jim knows I tell this story and he doesn't mind it. 1985 was such a great year for the Bears...and you remember one game that I really think was the catalyst. It was the third game, and it was on a Thursday night against Minnesota. You'll probably remember it as the greatest-coached game in the history of the NFL. You're going to remember that I held Jim McMahon out until midway in the third quarter until we got down by nine points. Then I got very smart and put him into the game and he threw three touchdown passes and we won the game. Then we came back to Soldier Field to play the Washington Redskins and we beat them 45-10, and Jim McMahon throws four touchdown passes. He completes 75 percent of his passes and there's no turnovers. This guy, for two weeks, he's the best quarterback in football, and nobody can argue that point. Then, you may not remember, but the next week we go to Tampa Bay to play the Bucs, and Jim overthrew Willie Gault for two touchdowns. He fumbled and lost the ball twice, and he threw three interceptions. We're behind by 10 points at halftime. We come into the locker room, and I'm not a guy who minces his words. I walked up to Jim and I said, "You stink." He didn't say anything. But he just kind of looked at me and it made me so darned mad and, of course he had those stupid sunglasses on. I said, "Jim, can you explain to me how you can be the best quarterback in football for two weeks and now for one half you're the worst?" He never said a word. He just looked at me. I said, "Jim, you're either ignorant or apathetic," and he just kept looking at me. Finally, I said, "Jim, which is it? Are you ignorant or apathetic?" Well, he kept looking at me and then he said, "I don't know and I don't care." 6/15/87

BEER, FANS, COMMERCIALS, & PARTYING WITH VIKINGS

For all the individuals whose feeling are hurt, maybe we'll have a big party at the end of the year and I'll buy them all a beer. 10/30/89

Asked if the Bears would consider using a no-huddle offense:
I've considered it, but every time I consider it, my coaches say, 'Let's go get a beer.' 9/7/89

...this is a different era. If I walk into a lounge the night before a game and a player's in there having a beer, what am I gonna do? Fine him? So he goes to his room and has a beer. Heck, we have beer at our team meal on Saturday nights. We didn't have any beer in 1963. You make up all sorts of rules, and it just creates rebellion. You have to be flexible. You can't legislate the way you used to. This team is loosey-goosey, yeah. But when it comes time to play on Sunday, they're ready. I don't worry about all the other stuff. 1/12/86

Does he look forward to the Platteville team picnic each year during camp?
The picnic is the highlight of my whole summer. The only thing that can beat that is a hole-in-one, back-to-back. I'm looking forward at the picnic to the good pork. It won't be as good as the pork chops at Ditka's restaurant, 223 West Ontario. Nor will the entertainment be as good as the Grabowski Shuffle. But at $19.95, pick up your own copy and take a look at it. I got all my commercials in. 8/12/87

SAINTS HUMOR

After his first victory as the Saints coach I would like to tell you that this all came to me in a dream. But I haven't been sleeping enough to dream. 9/24/97 *New Orleans Times-Picayune*

Asked by a reporter if Saints offensive coordinator Danny Abramowicz would keep six receivers on the Saints roster:
It would be very unlikely. Unless we become Air Abramwicz. The Polish Airline. 8/26/97 New Orleans Times-Picayune

When asked by a female Saints fan who the most gorgeous player was, Ditka replied that he didn't know because:
I spend all my time looking at their asses.
7/17/97 New Orleans Times-Picayune

Diana Ditka about going to a party that owner Tom Benson had for Ditka on his yacht:
Mike wasn't going to go, because he doesn't like boats. I said, "Mike, you have to go. It's for you." He said, "It's not for me." But Mike called me early this morning and said, "We have to go, because it's for me." 10/18/97 *New Orleans Times-Picayune*

During the Saints-Bears game Ditka was the subject of intense TV coverage How'd you notice?
They only had 38 cameras on me. My brother called me and told me if they had three more cameras on me, you'd get me (going to the bathroom) and eating. 10/8/97 New Orleans Times-Picayune

After Saints owner Tom Benson kissed Ditka on the sidelines in the final minutes of the Saints victory over the Cardinals:
I'm just glad I didn't have my dress on.
12/18/97 *New Orleans Times-Picayune*

HOW BAD ARE THE SAINTS, REALLY?

I think I've seen worse teams perform better by accident on offense. You can draw [plays] up in the dirt and make it work better than we make it work. 10/27/97 New Orleans Times-Picayune

It would be nice to play St. Augustine High School [in New Orleans] this week. But we don't have them on the schedule.
10/26/97 New Orleans Times-Picayune

I thought we had hit the floor, but we dug deeper.
10/27/97 New Orleans Times-Picayune

THE PSYCHOLOGICAL ASPECTS OF PRO FOOTBALL

The Name of the Game in the NFL: Winning

Wrong is not winning, that's all. 12/13/89

If you have a goal and it's important enough to you, you won't let anything deter you from the big picture. The big picture is winning and winning championships. 11/17/85

There is a tremendous amount of emphasis placed on winning, but if you're asking me if it's right, it has to be right.
12/30/86 *Chicago Sun Times*

I'd be foolish if I stood up and told you I didn't think we're going to win [the Super Bowl], because I don't think that way. I always think we are going to win. 1/14/86

It's all for the taking. Competition is what I've always loved. If you want it, baby, come get it. 10/17/97 *New Orleans Times-Picayune*

15

LOSING

I really believe this: If you accept defeat, then you're going to be defeated a heckuva lot more than you're going to win. You can be gracious in defeat, but boy, I'll tell you what, you can be gracious on the outside, but you better be doing flip-flops inside. If you're not churning and turning you're going to go out and get your butt whipped next time out. 11/17/85

If you lose, it's contagious. Last time out of the box we got beat pretty good [against the 49ers in the playoffs]. I think you try to dispel that as quickly as possible. 8/9/85

There is a tendency in football and anything in life for the head guy to point the finger at guys under him. When things go wrong, you don't have the production or respect. I've never done that. I never would do that. Part of that is that I'm not good at firing people. I'm not saying that wouldn't happen. But I not only have confidence in everyone of my staff [in New Orleans], but I happen to like them very much as people. I repect each one of them. And I think they're all good coaches. 12/28/97 New Orleans Times-Picayune

PLAYER COMMITMENT

The three most important things that matter are what you do in the meetings, what you do in practice, and what you do on the field in the games. The rest of it, well, I just look back to when I was a player. Discipline is important, and I'm tough on these guys, but that doesn't mean people shouldn't be people. These guys bust their tails for me, let them be themselves. The Chicago Bears aren't a reflection of my personality, they're a reflection of themselves. Maybe this league has been a little staid, a little regimented. I don't know. What the heck, if a guy is a minute late to a meeting well, then, maybe we'll go a minute longer. That's the way to do it, and if it isn't right, well maybe I will find out in time. But football is people. It's not selling clones and images. It's selling people. Heck, I'm not exactly the image of an NFL coach. I'm not over there on the sidelines, wearing glasses, my arms folded, looking studious, am I? 12/16/85

Player respect:

I guarantee you that you are not going to win unless the players respect what each other is doing. They figure that if a guy isn't pulling his load and they don't say something to him, then they are wrong. Because I'm going to say something to them. I am not going to say it in front of the media or the whole team anymore. But I am going to go in and say: "Hey, listen. We need this out of you and we need better play in this area." And I have done this with a few guys. But I think the players have to respect the players they are lining up with all the time. If they don't, then I think you've got some problems. 10/24/90

There's got to be a sense of urgency at all times when you play this game, until the game is over. Then you go on your merry way. Your mind has to be totally into what you're doing. You have to understand that one play, whether it is a good one or a bad one, can make the difference in a football game. I really believe that. And it's hard to get across to people. 12/9/97 *New Orleans Times-Picayune*

CONFIDENCE

If you're competing your confidence level should be pretty good. If it's not, be something else. Be a house painter. I have no sympathy for people in life who quit. You can have them. 12/9/86

I think sometimes in sports, you start looking for the other guys to make the plays. The other guy to shoot the basket or the other guy to hit the home run or the other guy to make the interception. You can't do that. You have to believe that you can make the play. 11/5/92

I don't think anything is unrealistic if you believe you can do it. I think if you're determined enough and willing to pay the price you can get it done. 9/8/85

A certain amount of confidence and cockiness is not bad. You don't want to get to the point where you roll the helmets out and think somebody is going to be scared to death of you. But I think being sure of yourself and feeling good is not a bad thing. 10/15/85

I tried thinking last week, "What if things don't go right on Sunday?" And I couldn't even think about it. I didn't even think it was a possibility. I'm not saying that out of conceit; I'm saying that out of confidence in this football team. 1/14/86

I think when you believe in yourself, automatically things get better for you. 8/28/87 *Chicago Sun Times*

PLAYER MOTIVATION

Ditka explained he wanted aces on his team:

A *for attitude. Players who want to achieve and want to win.*

C *for character. I don't care how much physical activity a man has, he has nothing unless he has character.*

E *for enthusiasm. You have to be enthusiastic, excited about your opportunities. If you are a pessimist and think bad things, those bad things are apt to happen. 2/10/82*

I'm gonna learn what motivates each of them. I'm gonna make them look at this [Super Bowl ring] and ask them if that's what's important. Yes or no. Or is it the paycheck that's most important? Because if it is, I'll tell them that there are a lot of places in this world where they can get a paycheck. I want people who are going to work for the team. Team pride has to be established. If it takes pulling out the '63 championship film, I'll do it. 1/24/82

If you take the time a player is truly in motion in a game, put the clock on it, I think the total action time is somewhere around 4 minutes and 10 seconds. That's not a lot to ask for a player's utmost concentration. 11/19/87

I just want everyone to play as hard as they can. I'm not saying I want everybody to play as good as they can, because I realize that is not a reality. Playing as hard as you can is always a reality. That means hustling, working, never quitting on the field, never giving up on anything. 10/11/91

On motivating veteran players:

I told them yesterday: "What you did last year or five years ago doesn't matter. Nobody cares. The game of life is based on proving yourself every time you go out in the marketplace. This is the marketplace." They've got to prove themselves today, tomorrow, the next day, this Sunday, and if they do that, they've got to get ready to prove themselves again, because the competition isn't going to get any easier. 8/6/91

Motivation in life comes from within. It's when you have enough resolve to say: "I'm not going to do this; I'm not going to do that." And quit whining and babying yourself. That's when you have it. Until then you don't have it. 11/29/91

You can design anything you want to do. If you coach well enough and get the players to believe enough in what you are doing and they really take it on the field and make it happen, you really have something going. 10/12/92

You don't have to love everybody you play with, but I think you've got to respect them. You've got to respect them for their work ethic and the way they play and the effort they put into it. You may not want to go out socially with them, you may not think the same politically, you may not think the same about a lot of things. But you have to respect the way they play the game. 8/10/92

After a disappointing 4-6 start in 1992:

I think I motivate as well as any coach. As a matter of fact, I'm not sure I don't motivate as well as any coach in football ever has. That is a bold statement to make, but I am making that statement. 11/19/92

If you really understand motivation, it is a personal thing. It is called guts, heart, and desire. It is not what a coach, manager, or a CEO can pour into people. You can give them direction and you can give them guidance. You can tell them what to do, when to do it and how to do it. If people don't do it or don't want to do it, they will never do it. Motivation is personal. 11/20/92

I heard Lou Holtz once say a smart thing about motivation. He says he gets rid of those who don't want to be motivated. There's something to that. The most important thing in any person being motivated is that person. It's foolish to say words motivate or an idea motivates. To a degree, it might. But the individual must feel he wants to achieve the ultimate he can with the talent he has. And he must bust his butt. He must be relentless in his pursuit to find excellence. To be the best. To find quality. That will never change. Motivation is probably the most overused word in the world, especially when they talk about coaches. 9/27/92

MOTIVATING THE SAINTS

Motivation is a word. Its nothing you can give people. The greatest motivation comes from within, from self-driven individuals who have great pride and a great feeling of achieving. I can tell them what's important. I can tell them what has to be done, why it has to be done, when it has to be done and how it has to be done. But they've got to do it. I know what's important. I know what it takes to succeed. I know how you do it. I know the price you have to pay because I've been there on every level. But they still have to do it. That's my job and our job as coaches. 8/24/97 *New Orleans Times-Picayune*

I explained to them what would happen if they were [unemotional], but maybe they don't believe me. I think they believe me. I think they know what I'm talking about. I don't want it to be false enthusiasm or less than genuine what they're doing. If the enthusiasm and emotion isn't real and the excitement isn't theirs, I don't want it. 10/1/97 New Orleans Times-Picayune

You can motivate greater with fear than with love. But I also motivate with love. It's a little different (returning to coaching) than I thought it would be. I didn't realize that it would be this tough mentally. You wrap your whole life up in 50 other people, plus some coaches, and there's a whole lot of pressure, because a lot of people are depending on the decisions you make.
9/28/97 *New Orleans Times-Picayune*

REALITY IN THE NFL

I believe very strongly in what I learned in 21 years in the National Football League. You have to work. You don't get to the top by dreaming. 2/10/82

We're in this game to win. When we cease to win, we cease to be, as a player or a coach. You lose enough, you're gone. It doesn't matter why. 10/25/89

On college players leaving school early for the NFL draft:
The American dream for a young man is to play well enough to get into college, do well enough in college to get out of college, and then when he is ready to come out, to go out make a lot of money then retire. That seems to be the American dream in baseball, basketball, and football. It's unfortunate that when kids sign to go to college that they are not honored as they are. The school makes a commitment; the individual should make a commitment. So everybody asks, 'Why does the NFL draft underclassmen'? I don't know. You'd have to ask the NFL. Evidently we're all afraid of lawsuits. Maybe we ought to face up to a couple of lawsuits and do the right thing instead of worrying about the wrong thing. 12/7/89

I just know in football there's a very thin line between this guy and the next guy. I learned a long time ago that nobody is indispensable. 1/5/86

Well, I'm a believer that you can't do a job if you don't show up to do it. Anybody can be replaced. I told them we'd be good with what we had; we'd be competitive with the guys who were there. At first they tuned me out. Maybe now most of them are convinced. 12/16/85

One person didn't make us Super Bowl champions, 45 people did. 11/27/86

We can't live on our past laurels. I can't live on what we did in 1986. No one cares that the Bears won the Super Bowl. They want to know what you did in 1987, 1988. 9/2/88

If you put loyalty ahead of talent you've got some problems. If we were 0-6, who'd be loyal to me? 10/16/86

You can't expect an organization to be mediocre. We all understand that as coaches. It's not a very secure job. If we don't win, we re gone. 12/30/86

You can't get fooled with the idea of experience and security. It's fine, but no amount of experience ever beat talent. 9/2/87

Any player who is not full speed and tries to play in the National Football League week after week, he's fooling himself. 11/11/91

Talent is not the most important reason you win in the NFL. It is the chemistry of how a team plays together. 11/15/91

You are supposed to beat certain teams, and you had better beat them. And there are certain teams that you are even with. You had better beat most of them. And there are certain games you are not supposed to win at all. You have got to win a couple of them. And that is the way to be a success. 11/19/91

It's a brutal business because a lot of people help make it brutal. Coaches are very expendable. Our job is to coach and to win. When you cease to win you're gone. It's a ruthless business...You're never remembered for what you've done. You're remembered for what you're doing right now. You're going to be counted for your last time at bat, not the fact you led the league in home runs three years ago. Nobody cares about that. 12/5/91

After winning his 100th NFL game:
It's fine, in life, when you get an individual honor. That's a great thing. There's no question about it. But the honors you get as a group or with a team or with an organization are the most important honors. 12/9/91

When you play professional sports, you're in a glass house. Everybody sees what you do; everybody analyzes what you do. The only way to curtail that is to do well. 10/18/92

On holdouts:
In life if you want to be somewhere, you go there. If you don't want to be there, you don't go there. I don't care about contracts or anything else. I went through that as a player and I understand. But if it's time to be somewhere, you get there. That's all there is to it. Get it done. Find a way to get it done. 8/6/91

On fans booing players:
There is nobody alive who has ever played sports who likes to be booed. Part of life is to be appreciated for your efforts and the job you are doing. When people don't seem to appreciate the job you are doing, it hurts... It would hurt you, it would hurt Babe Ruth. It would hurt anybody. 1/2/91

On gaining insights and secrets on other teams:
We don't ask any other players we bring in from another team any thing about what they do. First of all, we'd be surprised if they knew. Second of all, we don't want to confuse ourselves. 10/30/90

When asked about the likelihood of coaching in the NFL for more than 10 years:
A lot of coaches have proven you can. But what coaching over a period of time causes you to do is compromise areas I'm not willing

to compromise. Basically, it comes down to the players and the respect they should give the game. If I see that not happening, I can't be very tolerant with them, so I get into a bind. I want to get rid of the S.O.B.'s, no matter if they're still of value to the team or not. And that's a problem I have. So it becomes harder for me to condone certain things. I don't know if that's the problem Madden or Walsh had, but that's the problem I have. I have too much respect for the game to have someone take it lightly or flippantly or think this thing is going to be here forever for everybody. It's like stealing as it is. 10/29/89

Short-lived Super Bowl celebration:
For one moment in time, you're the best. Unfortunately, two days after we won, the [Space Shuttle] blew up. It kind of put everything back in perspective. 6/29/97 New Orleans Times-Picayune

LIFE PHILOSOPHY

I think everybody in life needs discipline. People crave discipline. 1/21/82

You can do anything the mind wants to do. If the will is there, you do it. 9/6/82

If you're the kind of guy who always looks over your shoulder, chances are you'll end up back there. 11/27/86

CRITICIZING PLAYERS

I didn't think there was anything to clear the air about. But maybe some players took offense at being criticized. Maybe it'd have been better to go to them about it before the media, but people lost sight of the fact we can use the media as a motivator. It worked for us last year. It got us a Super Bowl. Last season would be good to remember in all this. The rewards of doing it, what it took to do. People pulling together as a team. 10/21/86

I have to get this out so [the Bears players] can hear it. Maybe money is enough for some guys. Maybe they don't need Super Bowls, they don't mean that much to them. They mean a lot to me. But if they are willing to compromise and say, "Well, I'll just take this" and settle for less than the ultimate prize that's what they'll get. It won't be the Super Bowl they get. Maybe it will be the Pro Bowl but who really cares about the Pro Bowl? 9/1/86

I don't need to pump up guys when they're not playing good. I need to tell them why they're not playing good and try to make those corrections. 10/20/86

My job is to pat on the back and kick in the butt. I'm not fooling anybody on this team. They know what my priorities are. And the only reason I'm doing it is because I love to win. 12/28/86

Praising Players

Everybody needs a little reinforcement once in a while. Sometimes it's my fault. You get two stubborn people involved and you forget what the heck you're doing. You say, "I'm going to be as stubborn as him" or then he says the same about you and then nobody's talking. It gets stupid. 12/28/86

The Price of Success

Success is about having and excellence is about being. Success is about having money and fame and endorsements. But excellence is being the very best you can be all the time. There's a beginning and end to everything. [Fame] came because we were world champions. When that ceases to be, it will end. Maybe in life you have to learn that firsthand before you take it from somebody who has been there. I've been there. I have a philosophy that for a lot of life you're part of the parade and for a lot of life you just watch the parade. I don't want to watch the parade. I want to be part of it for a few more decades. 11/5/86

Sports can be a cancer because it makes a person want to achieve things only for himself. It condones an I-Me syndrome. You look at people making $300,000 a year arguing about making $400,000. It gets a little out of proportion because they're thinking too much of themselves, and I did that myself, too. 1/24/82

Maybe what's happened in our organization is a fall-out from what happened six-seven years ago with some of those draft picks. There are a lot of people who contributed to our success who aren't here now. And there are a lot of people who've contributed to our success who don't get the credit. 12/30/86 *Chicago Sun Times*

If you are satisfied in life, you may as well pack it up. Once you're the fat cat who says "I got it all," and you're satisfied with the money you have, the success you have, the house you're in, it's all over. 1/2/87 Chicago Sun Times

Egos

In the 1987 camp, the New Orleans Saints arrived to scrimmage against the Bears for three days. Some people expressed concern that it would be hard to restrain players from both teams from going all out:
We just have to find a good tempo where it's not all-out. There's a lot of egos involved in football. You have to be careful that somebody's ego isn't hurt. That even happens when we're practicing against one another. If somebody thinks they're getting beat, they're going to go a little harder. Then the other guy will go a little harder. We'll talk with the Saints about what we want to see out there, but I think we can control it on the field. 8/10/87

When you get up and look in the mirror, you better know who you are. If you need someone to tell you who you are, whether you are a good kicker, you've got a problem. Because you'll never be a good kicker. Being good only comes from within. That's a bunch of [garbage]. We've got guys that go see psychologists ...you know who you are, or you don't know who you are. 12/10/91

THE PHYSICAL ASPECTS OF PRO FOOTBALL

Being Tough

Either we have the identity of being tough or we don't. We've got to find out. You have to be tough physically to beat these people (other NFL teams). You have to take them on. You have to have a chip on your shoulder. We just have to get more physical on the football field. We've got to be aggressive in every area. If things go wrong, they go wrong; you can't worry about it. You go after them the next play. 12/3/82

We didn't win very much. Then we got smarter. I don't think we retaliated in Green Bay when they came after us. Just played hard, aggressive football. That's what we have to go back to. You're going to get some cheap shots. You take them and the next time you get a shot at a guy, you hit them good and clean. It will all even out. 8/25/86

The game of football is still about blocking and tackling. Always had been, always will be. A lot of people get caught up in tricking people and trying to be geniuses. That's fine. You can trick people once in a while. But you better bloody people's noses once in a while, too. 8/24/97 *New Orleans Times-Picayune*

INJURIES AND CONDITIONING

The game is a tough game, a physical game. You don't like the injury aspect but it's part of the game. 9/25/86

When you're losing, injuries become magnified. If we were winning, a lot of [players] would be out there running around playing. I'm not blaming them. When you're losing, you get more injuries. 11/8/83

If they are not 100 percent, I'd rather keep them out of the game. I think that's a mistake that we make. Our guys are so competitive they try to go out there at less than 100 percent, and the only thing they can do is risk re-injury. 11/9/86

We've been fortunate. Maybe it's the way we do things. Maybe it's the fact that we hit more in training camp than most people that get us ready to play. We also haven't pushed the guys who haven't been well. We let them get well before they play again. 12/20/85

Nobody makes you do anything in life. It's a cop-out to say that you got bad advice from a doctor. Nobody ever put a gun to my head and made me play. It's a pride thing, and every individual is made up differently. 10/25/90

In the old days, it was not only the individual but I think it was management's philosophy that if you could take a [painkilling] shot, take the shot. That's not my philosophy, and it's certainly not the upstairs philosophy at all. 9/18/84

When you're taking the injuries, that means you're taking punishment. That's the way it is. When you're giving it and giving it, you usually don't get hurt. That's simple fact of life. I didn't invent it. That's the

way it is. The hitter doesn't get hurt as much as the hittee. That's
what I'm trying to say. 7/27/97 New Orleans Times-Picayune

FIGHTING, ARGUING, TAUNTING

As long as there is a number one and somebody is trying to knock
him off, you're going to have competition. Some things happen
outside the rules once in a while. It's unfortunate. Nobody is proud
of it. But it happens. 12/7/86

We don't encourage the fighting at all because it's against the rules.
But I think no matter what you tell a player, what happens in the heat
of the game is something that's a gut level thing. 12/23/84

On fights in the 1986 Bears-Cardinals Preseason game:
What they did to [tight end, Pat] Dunsmore was atrocious. They
should be in a gang in New York and learn what it's really like...
Kicking a guy in his groin when he is down. That is a lot of guts.
Supposedly these guys are high-paid athletes, guys who went to
college. 8/25/86

Usually when there is an altercation, the camera will come back to
you and the best thing you can do is beat the guy you're playing
against and really make a fool out of him. People are going to try
and instigate because we play tough and they'll try to get somebody
kicked out of the game. 10/28/85

This is a winning business. If you want to win and don't remember,
because a call was a call and you accepted it and went on. The coaches
might have commented to the league, but I don't remember the players
saying much ever. 11/7/89

On taunting and baiting by other teams:
We've got a class football team. We've proven that a lot of years.
The only thing when you talk, you've got to back it up. Our game is
to play, not to talk. 12/29/88

Football Strategy and Tactics

OFFENSIVE PHILOSOPHY

Consistently, you've got to be around 24 or 25 first downs a game and be in the 350-yard [total offense] range. Because if those two things happen, that means the third thing happens, too—ball control. You would hope that if it happens, points come with it. 11/1/91

The passing game:

Possession means something only if you can score and make the other team come back after you. It does no good to have the ball for 40 minutes and score only 13 points. You cheat your offense to a degree. That has been happening in the league. I believe in ball-possession with the running game, but it can also be effective with the short passing game. The end-all is: Do you score more points than the other team? 9/29/91

It's important whatever team scores first. Controlling is important only if you can put points up to go with it. 12/30/84

Our goal is to get 24 or 25 points on the board and say, "come and get us." I don't care if the defense is the best in the world, if you can't get more than 13 points, you aren't going to win, it's all over. 9/8/85

Being able to drive the ball consistently on short passes and run the ball is what the game is all about. The big plays will happen as often by improvisation as by design. If they happen by design, they often are set up by well designed little plays. 9/27/83

My philosophy involves multiple offenses with different sets, the object being to keep the defense off balance. 1/21/82

You take what the defense gives you. That has been our philosophy. 8/18/82

I'd like to put together games of 200 yds. running and 200 yds. passing. I don't care if we ever throw for 400 (yards). That never impresses me. It impresses me if we win, and you win by being consistent in those two areas. 9/30/86

RUNNING THE BALL

Our game is to run the football. 11/16/86

Teams that run 40 times win. When you start not doing that, you start winning games the way we're winning them, with heroics. 11/15/87

We got to the Super Bowl by running. How many touchdown passes did we throw in the Super Bowl? When you get past zero, tell me. 12/7/86

In football, I don't care how fancy people think it's supposed to be, or how many formations you have or how you throw the football, if you can't run the ball effectively, you're not going to be a good football team. 8/23/92

QUARTERBACKS

They [fans] never have a chance to see the second quarterback much. They really don't know what he can do. As a result, they feel when you put the second quarterback in, you're really dealing at a tremendous disadvantage. I don't see it that way because if you keep 45 men and you don't really believe they can line up and play for you, then you've made a mistake. 11/24/85

Losing the quarterback:
You look at the teams that have lost their quarterback. Not saying that they can't win with other quarterbacks, because they can—some of those backups quarterbacks are great football players—but when you lose a quarterback, it does something to your system. 11/11/91

It's the hardest position to play in football, very few can play it effectively. It takes a supporting cast to do the job properly. Fans are the most amazing thing I've seen. They have heroes one day and make them bums the next. That shouldn't be. 12/5/91

You can't prepare for a quarterback in a system. You have to prepare for the system. 10/22/92

There is going to come a time when the blocking breaks down and the quarterback must run the football. And if it means he's got to put his head down and run over somebody, you've got to do that. Period. That's cut and dried, also. 10/26/89

TIGHT END

If the tight end is used properly, he can be very instrumental, maybe the most instrumental guy in the offense. 9/8/85

THE OFFENSIVE LINE

You can have all the skilled people in the world, but if you don't get stronger up front you can't protect those skilled people, and you don't have time to use them. I know we need other positions. But again, I'm going to be as basic as I can. The game of football is won with people up front, believe me. 4/19/97 *New Orleans Times-Picayune*

The snapper is an important position, because if you don't have it, boy, you can do some silly things. The extra point can become the most exciting play in the game. I've been there before where you were afraid to look out there when the guy is snapping the ball. 8/20/97 New Orleans Times-Picayune

KICKING

...You don't win championships because of great kicking games if you don't have anything else. 10/18/83

Defense

You win with good defense. Championship teams that I played on and the one I coached were basically headed up by great defenses. You have to be able to strike fear into people. You have to have an ability to score points and make first downs. But you do it with defense. 4/20/97 New Orleans Times-Picayune

We're going to try to be a very no-nonsense type of football team. We're going to try and exert as much pressure as we can defensively on our opponent. And we're going to try to put as much pressure as we can on the opponent's quarterback as we can without defense. We intend to be a multiple-front defense and a multiple-coverage defense. 1/29/97 *New Orleans Times-Picayune*

If we can play a base defense well, when the time comes to out-maneuver and out-trick people, we ought to be able to do a good job. 8/4/86

To me, defense is stopping the other guy when you have to stop him and making turnovers. Yardage doesn't mean beans. 10/3/85

You win with defense. You keep replacing defensive players. Defensive guys wear out quicker. When you look at all the great teams that have gone downhill—the Dolphins, the old Chiefs, the old Vikings—when the defense went, they went. 11/18/87

THE DEFENSIVE LINE

Your defensive line is important because if you don't have a pass rush, I don't care how good your [secondary] coverage is, you're going to get hurt. 8/10/92

The emphasis on sacks has ruined the (defensive) game.
2/14/97 *New Orleans Times-Picayune*

CORNERBACK

At cornerback, you've got to know when to suck it up and bite and gamble. If you sit back and worry about how good the receiver is, you're going to get intimidated and get your butt kicked. Go out there and shoot the gun, take the shot. 10/26/89

Player Personnel

When you build a team concept, you suppose everybody wants to think the team is the most important thing. That's ridiculous, because they won't think the team is the most important thing; they're always going to think the individual is the most important thing. My job is to try to get them—in the process of making them the most important thing—to play the best they can... 10/29/89

Whether people want to say that I'm too hard on a guy or I shouldn't get mad or I should get mad... It doesn't matter. What matters is what happens on the other side of the white lines. And that is played by the players. 10/6/92

There are a lot of coaches who believe you can't win with young people...You've got to go with those old, veteran players. Those salty dogs. I've been around too many teams that got old. 9/4/89

On coaching young players:
They don't assume that they know anything and they just go out and they try to learn. It's more fun because now when you tell them something there is a genuine interest in learning and not telling you what should be done. 10/23/88

THE NEW BEARS COACH

After 19 straight years of frustration, the Chicago Bears football team had failed to win a championship. Chicago Bears owner, George Halas, searched for a new head coach who could reestablish the pride and toughness of the glory years when the Bears were considered the Monsters of the Midway. The lethargic Bears needed a head coach who was skilled as a football tactician as well as a skilled motivator and Halas would not settle for less in his new head coach.

In the Chicago media, speculation as to who the new Bear head coach would be centered around four candidates:
George Allen, John Robinson, Mike White, and then assistant Dallas Cowboy coach, Mike Ditka.

Mike Ditka was asked by the Chicago media how he felt about being considered for the Bear job:
I'm very interested, but I deal in reality. There has been no direct contact between me and the Bears. But I assume they are interested in me because Mr. Halas has indicated to our people [the Dallas Cowboys] that he wants to talk to me. 1/8/82

In the Dallas Cowboy organization at least one person, General Manager, Tex Schramm, knew how badly Mike Ditka wanted the Bear head coaching job when he told Chicago reporters:
His ties are so strong to Chicago I think he'd welcome the opportunity to live with whatever problems there are. 1/17/82

In the previous football season, during a nationally-televised Cowboy game, Mike Ditka, in an act of frustration, threw a clipboard into the air. Reporters asked Ditka if he felt he had the right temperament to be a head coach in light of the clipboard throwing incident. Ditka shot back:
I'm 42 years old and I've been in pro football for 21 years as a player and coach. So I threw a clipboard once on national T.V., so what? I've been involved in a lot of football games and I throw one clipboard and it gets written about. 1/8/82

Ironically, years later Jim Dooley (Bear Director of Research and Quality Control) revealed that in George Halas' eyes, this incident was a key factor in Halas' decision to hire Ditka as the new Bear head coach:
Halas' secretary, Ruth, told me Halas was watching a Bear game at Dallas on T.V. with her when there was a close-up on camera of Ditka, then assistant coach for the Cowboys, storming and ranting on the sidelines. This was in 1981 when the Bears lost to them... Halas turned to Ruth and said, "That's my coach, that's who I want." 11/16/86

On January 20, 1982, George Halas announced:
For some time I have been working out a game plan designed to bring a winning football team back to Chicago. Now with the signing of Mike Ditka as head coach, phase one of that plan is complete... I like his ability to handle himself and other people and I know he'll do a good job getting people to play according to his desires. 1/21/82

In one of Mike Ditka's first press conferences he displayed his honest and open style in dealing with the media. He candidly assessed his situation as the new head coach:
I'm excited yeah, but I'm also realistic. I know that if you don't produce, all these good feelings, all these best wishes quickly turn sour. 1/24/82

I believe everyone has a destiny in life, and mine is with the Chicago Bears. I'm going to give Chicago a winning football team, an interesting football team, and a football team that everybody is going to be proud of. 1/21/82

Finally, with typical Ditka candor, he summed up his situation as new head coach:
Now the talking's stopped. Now I've got to do the job. 1/24/82

REACTION TO DITKA'S HIRING

Tom Landry (head coach Dallas Cowboys):
Anytime you lose a coach it's tough. He knows your system and he's a part of you. Mike's been loyal and I'm very happy for him. Mike is ready just like Reeves (Dan Reeves, Denver coach) was ready. They've both been at it long enough. If Mike gets a break he'll be OK. 1/20/82

Luke Johnson (Ditka's former offensive coach with the Bears):
I think it's a good deal. He was always one of my favorites. He won't take any guff from anybody. He had the winning spirit. 1/20/82

Fuzzy Thurston (former Packer guard):
If anybody can work for George Halas, Mike Ditka can. It's a difficult job, but Mike is tough enough to handle it. 1/20/82

Tom Brooksheir (former Eagle defensive back and broadcaster):
I went to Lake Forest last summer to watch a Bear workout and I didn't find the same intensity you get when you visit Philly or Dallas. But this will change under Ditka. Absolutely. The players will have to pay to get to the water bucket. 1/20/82

Earl Morrall (former Colt quarterback):
Ditka? Watch out for the Bears, if they've hired Ditka. It means they're going back to the mean old brawling Monsters of the Midway. 1/20/82

Joe Schmidt (former Lion linebacker):
Ditka will do a great job. If the Bears all play like Mike played they've got a winner. 1/20/82

Ditka: The Spirit of George Halas

Jim Dooley [Director of Research and Quality Control for the Bears] commented on Ditka's coaching style during a Tampa Bay/Bear game:
I saw a man with fist raised jumping out on the field, and I jumped back as if it was an apparition. What I saw in Ditka doing these things was the Halas spirit, Halas was there. It's eerie, Halas had bad hips. Mike has bad hips. But I always say to Mike that Halas would have still outrun him if they were the same age and they had their bad hips together. I don't know. Maybe not. Neither one could accept losing. Violent men, good men. 11/16/86

BEAR FOOTBALL DEFINED

We play a brand of football that threatens people at times. We're not going to intimidate everybody; but we're going to intimidate some people with the way we play. 9/8/85

He [Halas] always had a term he called "Bear Football." I think that's important... It's a type of football played on more than talent. It's played on heart and pride. 1/25/86

We give no quarter and ask none. 1/26/86

[We] want to be the best of all time. When you talk about the best of all time, that's something special. That's what we're shooting for. Anytime we deviate from it, we've got to get back on track. 10/13/86

I've seen guys come and go. I've seen the big mouths, the crybabies, the complainers, guys who don't want to pay the price. Those guys usually wind up on the outside looking in. The players that were moved out, it was because they were no longer playing Bear football. 9/1/89

We're arm tackling. We're reaching, we're grabbing. We're hoping. We're not doing a good job. That's apparent. And I don't like that because that's not the way the Bears became the Bears. The Bears became the Bears because we challenged people. 9/2/88

KEEPING THE SPIRIT ALIVE

I took this job not because it's head coaching. I took it because it's the Bears. Tough. Like George Halas. I didn't understand what he was all about when I was a young punk playing for him. But I do now. This is the best job in the world. 12/4/84

What you do in life by yourself doesn't mean as much as what you accomplish with a group of people. It's because of Mr. Halas that I'm here. I'm just trying to pay some dues. 1/27/86

On Halas' play — "The quarterback sneak:"
I'll still call it and I'll call it again and I'll call it again. If I don't, Mr. Halas will roll over in his grave. 10/6/86

Look, if George Halas was coaching this team you know what he
would do with the Super Bowl Shuffle? He'd take a copy of it, call
a team meeting, then put it on the floor and jump all over it. 1/12/86

*Everything we do is dedicated to him [Halas] as long as I'm here.
When I'm not here, they can dedicate to anybody they want to, but
it's dedicated to him as long as I'm here. 1/6/85*

**Johnny Morris [sportscaster and former Bear] was asked when
he last saw Ditka cry prior to Vanisi's firing. Morris answered:**
Probably when Halas died. 1/16/87 Des Plaines Daily Herald

*The gratifying thing about this [success] is when people ask me what
it means, it means one thing: I've repaid a confidence [to Halas].
11/17/85*

THE DEATH OF GEORGE HALAS

I feel very bad about it. But the sport of football and the city of
Chicago should feel bad because of what he has meant to the city,
and what he has meant to the sport. Whether you always agreed with
Mr. Halas or not, he is the reason the league is what it is today. The
contributions he has made to this city are unbelievable also. 11/1/83

*I hadn't talked to him in a couple of weeks. Before that, I had talked
to him quite regularly. As a matter of fact I had seen him quite
regularly before that. The improvement he had made since March or
April, when he had the bad time, was phenomenal. He was very
enthused about everything. Very up on everything. He wanted to
talk about players, the team, and was still very much involved mentally
in everything. 11/1/83*

LOOKING BACK

On contract sessions with Halas:
I never expected to win, to get what I asked for, but it was a great
experience. 11/2/83

What's the difference between Halas and Ditka?

The difference is that when he [Halas] said something to the officials, they listened. When I say something, they don't listen. 11/2/83

On his salary:

That has never been a concern. When I came here [in 1982], when Mr. Halas hired me, he didn't pay me a lot of money. A lot of people said, "You're crazy." And I said, "I'm not crazy because if I win it won't matter and if I lose it won't matter, either, because I won't have a job." 12/12/90

You've got to understand that we have won, but I haven't won. It is not me, it is our organization, our coaches. I think it is about time somebody has started talking about what a great job [head of player personnel] Bill Tobin has done over the last eight or nine years. It has very little to do with me except that I understand this: When we win I get a lot of credit and when we lose I get the blame. There is no problem with that. 12/16/90

DITKA ON MIKE MCCASKEY, HALAS' GRANDSON

Mike McCaskey was named new Bear president
in 1983, Ditka was positive about the selection:

Mike is a bright, sharp, young guy. His thoughts on winning are the same as mine and Jerry's [General Manager Jerry Vainisi]. Mike will make progressive changes, not changes for the sake of change. 11/12/83

What does Ditka think of Mike McCaskey?

He's a fine man, and he's my boss. 6/15/87

After the firing of Jerry Vainisi in January of 1987, Ditka
was hurt and visibly upset. On McCaskey's role in the firing:

I learned as a kid the guy who owns the ball and bat can call the game anytime he wants to. So I accept that.

1/21/87 *Des Plaines Daily Herald*

MᶜCASKEY ON DITKA

But just because we're perceived as opposites doesn't mean we can't operate well as a team. On the contrary, the meetings we've had with all our people have been extremely good. Jerry Vainisi, Bill Tobin, Mike and I have a strong relationship. 12/4/84

I like Mike. I admire him as a man. It's a good working relationship. Both of us know the other has an enormous pride in the Bears being the best. The fact we're different personalities is good in that respect, not bad. People think you need personalities that are alike to be successful. I disagree. The strongest team, management or football, has a diverse set of characters. 9/15/87

I found out that we both share a respect for what a lot of people call old-fashioned values. That work, effort, character and heart mean as much as anything else. Everybody knew he was a motivator. The question was always raised about his football smarts. This is a savvy and clever football coach, who will do the smart thing. 11/17/85

The head coach is in charge of the offense and defense. It's up to him to set up the dynamics. He has complete charge and control. I won't interfere. 11/12/83

It's absolutely critical that the head coach be one who will bring tough, aggressive and smart football, and by the way, the Bears have played this year and in prior years; the job Mike Ditka and his coaching staff have done has shown that's the kind of team we are going to have. 1/3/85

Mike McCaskey on his relationship with Mike Ditka in 1988:
I would say we have a very good relationship. We are both fully committed to making the Bears Super Bowl champions. We have worked out a distinctive philosophy for who the Chicago Bears are in the 1980s. 11/30/88

McCASKEY ON FIRING VAINISI

**On January 10, 1987 Bear president Mike McCaskey
stunned Chicago by firing Jerry Vainisi, Bears General
Manager and Mike Ditka's best friend. A few days later,
McCaskey was asked if Mike Ditka would leave the Bears
at the end of the 1987 season. McCaskey replied:**
*I don't think so. I told Mike all season and I'll tell you publicly, that
he's done a fine job as head coach of the Chicago Bears. I hope and
expect he'll have a long career as head coach of the Chicago Bears.
1/16/87*

I have to really want him [Ditka] to be head coach too. There's too
much at stake to do it differently than I'm doing it. Ditka wanting to
be head coach is what's important about the way the decision gets
made. 2/1/87

McCASKEY SUMS IT UP

First of all, I think Mike Ditka has done an outstanding job being the
head coach of the Chicago Bears and I look forward to his being the
head coach for a lot of years to come. I think everything's going to
work out just fine. I think he does want to be the head coach here. I
think he has Chicago Bears blood running through his veins. I think
he's excited about what the future holds as far as our being able to
make a real strong run at several Super Bowls, and I think he wants
to be a part of it. 4/5/87 *Chicago Sun Times*

VAINISI ON DITKA

*From the very start, Mike Ditka has been unbelievable. In camp I
would brief him on the status of Bell and Harris. He never complained
at not having them. He said don't compromise, we'll go with what
we have. 1/8/86*

He [Ditka] was very confident last year. I think he's gained even more confidence in himself, his program, and the club. I think he believes stronger than ever that it's a team sport and we don't rely on any one individual. He's got to try to convince everybody that the quarterback is another guy out there. 1/3/87 Des Plaines Daily Herald

He's just more a complete coach. I think this was his greatest coaching challenge this year—having the injuries we had coupled with the changes that occurred in the off season and having to coach a defending championship team. 1/3/87 Des Plaines Daily Herald

DITKA ON VAINISI

On the early Bears years:
I didn't have anybody in my corner except Jerry Vainisi. Everybody else had the magnifying glass out and they were looking really hard. 11/17/85

Ditka on Vainisi being fired:
Fellas, I really thought that I wasn't going to say anything but I don't know that that would be totally fair to anybody concerned. But I'm going to just say a very brief statement, and because I think it's a situation which I am not really entitled totally to comment on. Let me just say that I was totally taken by surprise, totally. And I was very, very hurt. Jerry Vainisi is respected in our business as one of the best. And he deserves that because he's earned that. He was called upon to take this job by coach Halas, as I was. And I think that's probably the reason we're so close. I deeply respect that. It was his [Halas'] last wish that Jerry Vainisi be the general manager and that I be the coach or it would have been changed. We've worked together the best we can. We've tried to do things intelligently to put a football team on the field that the people in the city of Chicago could be proud of. And I think we've done that. What hurts me the most is that he [Vainisi] is my best friend. And I and the players on the Chicago Bears are gonna miss him very, very much. I wish him the best that you could wish for losing a best friend. And he'll land on his feet, believe me, because he's good at what he does. I feel

very, very sorry for his wonderful family, his children, Doris [Vainisi's wife], his parents, who have really lived and died with him with the Chicago Bears because it has become a major part of his life. You just don't cut off an appendage from your body and then go on and live normally. As I say, Jerry Vainisi's a class person and he'll end up in good shape. I really don't have anything to say.
1/10/87 Chicago Sun Times

THE BEARS ORGANIZATION ON DITKA

Dick Stanfel, offensive line coach:
I think he tried to control himself more [in 1986]—his personality on the field. I think he realizes that sometimes he gets excited and pulls somebody who's not at fault and shouldn't be pulled. I think he's adjusted to that by apologizing to them and telling them. He's not afraid to tell them he's wrong. Every year I think you mature more and more in your job. He's done an excellent job in what he's doing—by his motivation and by his coaching. I think he's one of the top guys in that. 1/3/87 *Des Plaines Daily Herald*

Bill Tobin, Vice President, player personnel:
He's a joy to work with, he's not afraid to listen. 11/17/85

Steve Kazor, special teams coach:
He's kind of a person as a head coach who depicts what a guy is supposed to be. He knows how to positively reinforce people and negatively reinforce people, and gets the most of them.
1/3/87 *Des Plaines Daily Herald*

Ed Hughes, offensive coordinator:
In the back of Mike's mind, he has a lot of Landry in him. Tom worried that the defense would get a scheme on you. He always wanted to keep them from having that perfect defensive scheme.
9/27/86

Dick Stanfel:
Mike Ditka is the rod, and I'm the smoother-over. He gets on the [offensive] line. I don't blame him. It's his team. I'm the one who has to smooth it over and say, it takes time for people to get timing and coordination. 8/13/87

Vince Tobin, when asked if it bothered him
when Ditka yells at him on the sidelines:
I try not to, but I don't know if you ever get used to it. The big thing is you've got to continue to go ahead and call the defenses. The plays go on. 12/8/87

Greg Landry, quarterback coach:
I think one thing [Ditka's] looking for by maybe allowing one of the offensive coaches to call the plays is that now he can keep involved with both sides and we as an offensive coaching group can discuss it with the players. Why didn't the play work? Maybe someone didn't execute his assignment. Or maybe we should get off it because it's not good against their defense. We just need to communicate better on the sidelines and find out what's going on. We've got experienced players. They have a good understanding of what's going on. We need to use that knowledge in game situations.
1/24/88 *Chicago Sun-Times*

Vince Tobin on television coverage of
Ditka yelling at him on the sidelines:
I think when it happens that it undermines your authority as a coach when the players see it. We have talked about it. Mike's working not to let it happen again. Really, the main time it happened was in the second Green Bay game. He tries. But you're not going to change him. Mike's emotional and very, very competitive. He has a quick temper. What he wants is for every team to be shut out and not make a yard. That's how he is, and he is not going to change. I have a very good relationship with Mike, and I think he has total confidence in me. 1/8/88

Bill Tobin:
We lost 21-17 this year to Washington in the playoffs for a combination of reasons. But not because we were outcoached or outmanned. A dropped ball here, a poor pass here, a wrong route, a missed blocking assignment...little things. All it requires is some fine tune-ups. No overhauls. Just continue to add some new blood. That's my responsibility: to convince Mike Ditka and Mike McCaskey what players would be best for us and why they'd be best. We've done a good job in the past at it, and we plan to do a good job again. 2/5/88

JERRY VAINISI LOOKS BACK

Vainisi on Flutie:
I still think getting Flutie was the right decision, even though McCaskey and Tobin didn't agree. But McCaskey made the trade, not me. He asked me to find out what the Rams wanted for Doug, and that's all I did. Maybe it's true that the Bears would have beaten Washington [in the playoffs] if Mike Tomczak or Steve Fuller had started instead of Flutie. But getting Flutie was right because we didn't know if Jim McMahon would play again with his injury. Tomczak was having an off year, and Ditka had lost confidence in Fuller. Fuller had probably the worst year of his career. We had an excellent team, needed stability at quarterback, and I still don't think the decision to get Flutie was that outrageous.
11/20/87

Vainisi on his friendship with Ditka:
It sometimes paired us off against McCaskey and Bill Tobin. I'm sure that had an influence on McCaskey's decision. 11/20/87

Vainisi on Perry:
In the 1985 draft, McCaskey and I were anti-William Perry. We wanted Jessie Hester, the wide receiver who went to the Raiders on the pick after we took Perry. Tobin and Ditka wanted Perry and talked McCaskey and me into the decision. The Raiders would have taken Perry if we chose Hester. 11/20/87

Vainisi on the 1985 season:
We had a midpoint swoon in 1985, the year we won the Super Bowl. It's natural. It's hard for any coach to keep his team motivated every week. No one is pressing the Bears in the Central Division, and they're relaxing a little bit. Come December 1, Ditka will have them refocused and built up. I don't think this Bears team has as much depth as we had in 1985, but they're still the best team in the league. 11/20/87

The Future: Ditka and the Bears

I think you have to look at everything. I think we have to look at ourselves. I've been talking for a long time that this is what I want to do and I have to rethink myself, too. Because unless I have the control of what I'm doing, I don't want to do it anymore. I really mean that. That is essential to me. Right now I don't know. I feel like there are some things that are a little out of whack. I'm not blaming anybody, and certainly not feeling sorry for myself. But I think everybody has to get on the same page in the organization. Where we want to go, what kind of players we want to go there with, and how we are going to get there. Then we have to make a concentrated effort to get there. 12/21/92

When asked about the Bears becoming more active in Plan B and making trades and his discussions with club President Mike McCaskey:
If there is a difference (in opinion) then I think I would have to depart. We haven't talked about those things yet. 1/5/92

I'm going to make a decision, too. The only way I'll [continue coaching the Bears], is if I control it [offense, defense, and player personnel]. 12/21/92

On the Bear organization not letting the head coach hire and fire assistants:
If they don't work for me, then there's no use having a head coach. Just let the owner be the head coach. 12/22/92

My intention is to coach in 1993. That is my intention. If something would change that... I would have no control over what would change that. That is my intention totally. There are a lot of ways to get a job done, and I will find a way, if that opportunity is there. I think there will be changes that everybody will make, including me, I have all intention of coaching here in '93, and I think things will be done properly. 12/23/92

I was put here for a reason, and I have no regrets, no problem with anything that has happened over the 11 years. You're put in places for reasons. So if there's another place, another thing to do in life, we'll see what happens. One constant in life is change. I think they'll be changes for the positive. 12/24/92

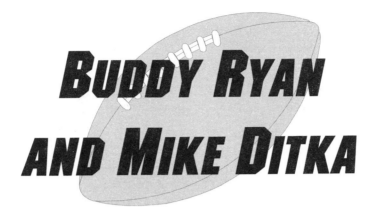

BUDDY RYAN AND MIKE DITKA

The Conflict

Buddy Ryan was the defensive coordinator for the Bears for eight years from 1978 to 1986, when he resigned from the Bears to become the head coach of the Philadelphia Eagles. Buddy Ryan was known as the architect of the famous Bears "46 defense" which led the league in defense in 1985 as well as helped the Bears to an 18-1 record and the Super Bowl Championship. Prior to Buddy Ryan's departure there had been rumors of a personality conflict between Ditka and Ryan. Until the drafting of William Perry, however, this conflict did not surface publicly.

FEUDING

Buddy Ryan:
He never had any authority over me. The man [George Halas] had hired me to coach before he hired him. Ditka took the job knowing the man had hired me to coach the defense. I mean he (Ditka) must have been happy to have the job or something. 9/29/89

**To Buddy Ryan's criticism of picking
William Perry in the draft, Ditka responded:**
Kinda makes me look like an idiot because I'm the guy that picked
him. 8/8/85

**A reporter commented that Ryan may have made negative
statements about Perry to motivate him. Ditka replied:**
*I'm not sure I believe in reverse psychology, but everyone has his
own way of doing things. I learned if you can't say good things about
people don't say a whole lot about them.* 8/8/85

Buddy Ryan's view:
Ditka and I get along fine. We might have a difference of opinion,
just like you and I might have a difference of opinion. I always get
tickled when I read Ditka and Ryan are fighting. I don't see it that
way and neither does he. But I guess it sells a lot of papers. 8/12/85

**As the Bears moved into the 1985 playoffs, they shut
out the New York Giants 21-0 in the first playoff game.
Next they shut out the Los Angeles Rams 23-0. This was
the first time a team had back-to-back shut out playoff
games. The Bears then defeated the Patriots 45-10 in
the Super Bowl. Ditka commented:**
*Our players had a mission, the defense, you gotta love them. The job
Buddy did was just great.* 1/26/86

THE BEARS REACT TO RYAN'S DEPARTURE

**Shortly after the Super Bowl Buddy Ryan accepted the head
coaching job with the Philadelphia Eagles. Ditka's response:**
I bet a lot of people thought I'd be looking for the highest building to
jump off of this morning. The challenge will be tremendous for us to
comeback. There will be a new dimension of Bears football. I think
everyone will like it. 1/30/86

Otis Wilson:
Well, it's no secret they didn't get along. It was in the papers all year. They're two pretty stubborn guys who say what they think. I just hope Ditka doesn't hire a yes-man now. I hope he doesn't want that. Buddy wasn't like that at all. And look how we wound up. On top. 1/30/86

Mike Singletary:
I lost two teeth at the dentist, my best friend and defensive coordinator... Just makes you appreciate the good times that much more, I guess. 1/30/86

Dan Hampton:
Everybody was close, with a common goal. Mike Ditka handled the offense, Buddy the defense, and we went all the way. I didn't really see any problems. We had the two best coaches in the NFL. Mike and Buddy. Now we've lost one. It'll be hard without him. Real hard. 1/30/86

Steve McMicheal:
Buddy was here for how long? Eight years? And we had the Number One defense the last two? Well, he's a real genius wasn't he? What about the first six? 9/14/86

RYAN AND DITKA REACT

Buddy Ryan:
[Ditka] wished me well and I'm sure he was sincere. Mike's a good man, regardless of all the stuff you read. Usually people would ask, "Buddy what do you think about this?" Then they'd ask Mike, "What do you think?" He doesn't give the same answer I do, so they say, "Oh, there's a disagreement." 1/30/86

Ryan:
Ditka didn't know what was going on, on defense and we cussed each other out, but we would do that every three or four weeks. 2/7/86

Ditka:

[Ryan] took a lot of bows and I let him take them; but he didn't let any of his assistants take any bows. Why doesn't [offensive line coach] Dick Stanfel get more credit? We led the league in rushing three years in a row. 2/7/86

BEARS 13 — EAGLES 10

Although the Bears won, it was obvious to all concerned that this wasn't just another game. Bear players noticed that Ditka wanted very badly to beat Ryan's Eagles. Walter Payton said:
One time on the field, I told our guys, "Come on let's play our type of game. Let's not get uptight like Mike is. Let's do what we do best and not let him affect us." 9/15/86

Ditka tried during the pregame interviews to downplay the personal aspect of the game. After the victory he explained:
I made it too much of a personal thing. You can try to do individual things and that's wrong. We're in a team sport and when I have to start thinking I have to rely on being a genius to win football games, I've got a lot of problems. 9/15/86

He [Ryan] has talked about the Super Bowl in three years, he'll be lucky to have a job in three years. 9/16/86

MORE FEUDING

Buddy Ryan's reaction to Ditka's heart attack:
Must have been gas. 12/30/88

Ditka's reaction to reports of Buddy Ryan's hospitalization November 30th for choking on a piece of pork:
Couldn't have been Ditka's pork chops [from Ditka's restaurant]. They're so tender, nobody could choke on them. 12/30/88

Prior to a 1988 playoff game between the Eagles and Bears in Chicago, Ryan was asked if he had spoken to Mike Ditka since he left the Bears:
Nope, I didn't even talk to him when I was there. 12/28/88

Asked about his relationship with Ditka, Ryan replied:
There never was a relationship between him and I. He's not my kind of people, anyway. I don't know anything about him, don't care to know anything about him. 9/29/89

Ryan on Ditka and his involvement in Bear personnel moves:
I didn't know he had the authority to get rid of anybody. I thought personnel people were the ones who did that. Maybe he does. He loves to give that impression...like he knows what he's doing in the draft, too. But he's out playing golf in the spring. How in the hell can he know anything about the draft? 9/29/89

Ditka's turn:
He's just jealous. You know what they say. Empty tin cans make the most noise. And he's an empty tin can. This game is between the Bears and Eagles, not Ditka and Ryan. We all know who would win that one. Ditka, hands down. 10/3/89

After another Bear victory over the Eagles in the 1989 regular season, a reporter pointed out to Buddy Ryan that he had lost all four times to the Mike Ditka coached Bears. Buddy replied:
Yeah, you don't lose that many times to anyone and stay in this league long. 10/3/89

Ditka on feuding with Ryan:
I'm the duck and it's like water off a duck's back. 10/3/89

McMahon, Perry and Payton

Jim McMahon, Rookie Quarterback

In McMahon's case, he is unusual. He's read defenses, he's hit outlet passes. When you throw 50 times a game [in college] you've got to do those things. It should be no problem for him. 5/2/82

Never entered my mind to take him out after the interceptions. Jim is never going to lose confidence in himself. He'd have to get hit by a truck. 11/22/82

Jim McMahon is the best quarterback. He's the quarterback of the future. He's the starting quarterback and will not come out unless he is injured. If the Bears are going to win, Jim McMahon will be the catalyst. 11/8/83

I've been around some veteran quarterbacks who don't handle themselves much better than Jim does. Sure he'll improve, but I'm saying he's doing the job as far as understanding and reading and moving out of the pocket. When he comes out of that pocket, he comes out with design. He doesn't come out in panic. He's looking for something downfield or looking to make something work. He knows what he wants to do. And when he runs, there is no indecision. He runs to make a first down or get as much as he can. 12/10/82

McMahon Speaks Up

I think I proved some things last year [1982] that I can play in this league. I proved it the first couple of games this year. In the Denver game he [Ditka] got real upset when I threw a couple of bad balls. It was not like I was just trying to give 'em back the football... I try to forget what has happened because everyone knows how Mike is. He's temperamental. We're the people who have to accept that. When he says something that could make you upset, he's saying it out of frustration. We've just got to understand. 11/1/83

We're still all playing fairly tense. We're not just loosening up and going out having fun. We're all just too worried about our jobs instead of playing with reckless abandon. We're worried about being replaced and we can't worry about it. 11/1/83

Ditka on Tough Guy, Jim McMahon

On telling McMahon to run out of bounds occasionally to avoid getting hurt:
Because of his competitive instinct, he's going to chafe about that. It runs contrary to everything he believes in. 8/11/85

Every play can't always be a great play. McMahon has had to learn this, just like Joe Montana had to learn it, and Joe Theismann and Roger Staubach. A quarterback has to live again to fight another day. 7/14/85

You won't intimidate him. It will just make him work harder if you get to him or frustrate or pressure him. He's a scrapper. He's not going to give up or quit on you. 1/1/86

He put his butt on the line out there.   The things he does nobody else does.   The hits he took, the running, the scrambling.   He's trying to make things happen, trying to do things for the football team, trying to get a first down by diving and sliding and jumping.   Other guys just aren't going to do that.   He plays it different.   10/27/86

He's some kind of gutsy guy.   10/27/86

He's fun and he's going to create excitement.   He'll put you people [the media] on a little bit and have a few laughs.   But he's a pretty good person.   I'll say he's a very good person.   He has a lot of qualities that are important to have, the way he treats his family and his kids and what's important to him. 1/25/86

FEUDING THE MCMAHON, DITKA WAY

Johnny Carson: Is McMahon crazy?
Mike Ditka: He doesn't like me because I happen to be the coach and there's a certain amount of authority there.
1/21/87 Chicago Sun Times

Jerry Vainisi on McMahon:
We just want Jim to realize that he has to do things Ditka's way. By that, I don't mean we want Jim to change one bit as a character, as being Jim. Ditka, when he was a player, lived on the edge a bit himself. So he understands. He doesn't care whether Jim wears a Boston College jersey to practice or any of that other stuff that makes Jim unique. Mike is very good that way, and I don't know of another coach in the NFL who allows his players to be individuals as much as Mike does. Mike puts up with a lot, but there's a point where even he might say, enough. I don't think that's going to happen with Jim. We'll learn if he's sincere about what he says this spring; when it's time to get ready for next season. But Jim's a winner, and I think he's upset with the way this season has gone. I think you'll see the same McMahon in training camp, only without the belly. 12/11/86

Jimbo Covert:

They're not two different personalities (Ditka and McMahon). I think they're almost the same personality. On old teams, they'd say if you fight with teammates or the coach, there'd be dissension. It seems like stuff like that brings us closer together. It's kind of weird, but it's the Chicago Bears, I guess. 8/19/86

Ditka on Jim McMahon:

[We'd] probably would be good friends if I wasn't the coach. We talk once every leap year. Jim doesn't respect authority. When I played, I spoke my piece and I didn't always agree but I respected authority. I'm an authority figure. That's my opinion. He might say something else. I'm sure he would. 3/19/87

McMahon:

We don't always agree on everything but I think he's [Ditka] fair. He'll let you know if you screw up, and that's the way it should be. There's no wishy-washy person in Mike and that's the kind of guy I like to play for. I don't like guys who tell you one thing and then go and tell somebody else another thing. He's not like that. He'll tell you to your face you screwed up or you didn't. It's the way it should be. 1/1/86

McMahon:

Well, I don't think our problems are as bad as they are made out to be. I just don't understand him all of the time. We had that talk recently and I figured everything was okay. Then, after that, he tells me at practice one day he doesn't believe I'm hurting as bad as I say I'm hurting. He says they are going to put me on the injured reserve list. I say go ahead, if that's what they want to do, but I didn't think I needed that much time. As it turns out, the shoulder separation didn't. It's healed. It's the other thing I hope Mike understands now. He's been sybilizing a lot lately with a lot of guys, not just me... You know, going through all different personality changes—like Sybil the girl in the movie. I don't know why he or anybody else would think that all of a sudden, I don't want to throw a football. 11/23/87

McMahon Bites Back

He [Ditka] keeps ripping me for not coming to camp in shape. Well I did more running this year than I did the last four years. And I'm down to 195 pounds. But I'm hurt and what's the use of playing hurt now? Why not get ready for the regular season? Is that so hard to understand? And nobody knows this body of mine, what it can do and when, better than me, right? Do I have to prove I can take pain all over again? Look at me. This ol' body is going straight to the Smithsonian when it's done with me. The leadership stuff, that's fine. But I don't think I've been all that bad as a leader. I've done everything I can to help us win. I've played with broken bones, a lacerated kidney, played whenever I could. I can't see why Ditka would start thinking I'm lazy now. I hope my teammates know I'd go through a brick wall for them and I know I'd go through a brick wall for them. Is that being lazy? Not caring? I mean there were other guys getting treatment Thursday. But did they get fined? Why me? 8/18/86

Impasse

Ditka:
We're going to have a meeting. I'd like to sit down and talk. I'm not mad at anybody. 8/18/86

McMahon:
A meeting? What happens if we have it and one of us doesn't come out of there? 8/18/86

The Acquisition of Doug Flutie

McMahon:
I doubt if [Ditka] will chew his [Flutie's] butt out the way he's chewed out Mike [Tomczak] or Steve [Fuller] or me. 10/16/86

Ditka:

Jim's the quarterback and he knows it. He has to carry us. But he hasn't been healthy. He's played in four of our seven games. At that rate, he'll play in nine of our sixteen. That leaves seven unanswered and we need insurance. 10/22/86

TRADING McMAHON

McMahon:

The conversation was short. He [Ditka] said, "We made a deal and you're going to San Diego. We appreciate all you've done for Chicago and good luck." 8/19/89

Ditka:

Dan Henning [Chargers coach] said, "Can he play?" I said you bet he can play. I think he needs a change of scenery. I think he needs to get away from Mike Ditka. 8/19/89

Steve Zucker, McMahon's agent:

It [McMahon's relationship with Ditka] deteriorated over the years and it really began in 1986 when Jim had that shoulder injury and the coach did not believe him. He finally needed shoulder surgery. Then last year when Jim didn't play in the Detroit game on his doctor's advice, that is what really got to Mike Ditka. It is Mike Ditka's team and Mike Ditka feels he can win no matter who is playing for him. So we'll find out. I think that anybody that knows Jim McMahon knows that he will play hurt. But evidently his coach had some doubts about that. 8/19/89

Ditka:

We decided to go in a different direction—I did—with young quarterbacks. It is an ideal situation for Jim to continue his career in a quality situation where he is going to be the starting quarterback. They want him to start; they don't want him to back up. I couldn't give him that guarantee. I just felt, after what I've seen, that it is time for us to move in another direction. These are tough decisions.

I don't like these decisions, but I know this, he has been instrumental in the success this club has had through the '80s. He has been a very colorful character. He has been loved by a lot of people and rightly so. This is probably a little tough on him. But in the long run, it will be the best situation for both organizations. 8/19/89

McMahon:
I don't think it was a football deal at all. We haven't gotten along for a couple of years. He doesn't like people to take away his spotlight. I was probably one of the guys, if not the only guy, who could do that in this town. So he got rid of his competition now. He would do that to spite me. 8/21/89

Ditka:
You've got to understand that I was young once, too. A lot of emotions run through you. I would hope he doesn't feel that way because I think that's silly. We've only tried to do the constructive things. Some of the things [McMahon said] are absurd. If he doesn't like me, that's fine. I happen to like him, I really do. 8/21/89

William Perry

WEIGHTY MATTERS

On William Perry:
The other guys in our division are sitting there wondering, "How are we going to control this guy?" I feel sorry for the centers, and for ours in practice. 5/1/85

Responding to criticism that William Perry might be too heavy to play in the NFL, Ditka explained:
The stuff about his weight is the biggest fallacy around. The important thing is his strength and stamina. Can we get him in shape? It's foolish to speculate on his weight. 7/14/85

THE BIGGEST BACK IN HISTORY

Bill Tobin:
From the first Mike Ditka and I thought, "Can you imagine tackling that guy?" When I saw Mike the week of the San Francisco game, I told him this might be the week. He smiled ...the night before the San Francisco game, he told me he put him [Perry] in. 10/30/85

Why did Ditka put William Perry in the backfield?
I just wanted to see if he could run with it. 10/14/85

Was giving the ball to Perry in the Bears 26-10 victory a payback to the 49ers for putting a 49er lineman in the backfield during the game the Bears lost to the 49ers the previous year?
You think I'd do that? I'm not that kind of guy. I wouldn't try to get one-up on people. I just don't forget very easily. 10/14/85

William Perry:
I was looking for the end zone. When the 49ers saw I was the ball carrier, their eyes got real big. 10/14/85

Ditka:
Gives you a little food for thought on the goal line, doesn't he? I mean, it's really something you've got to think about realistically. There's a chance that could happen. 10/15/85

The hilarious thing about this Perry thing is it's kind of busted the staid image in the NFL that all running backs are slender, six foot tall, between 185 and 215, and built. This has made a farce out of that. Every underdog in society relates to Perry. 11/17/85

SUPER BOWL HERO

William Perry:
I want to thank Coach Ditka for letting me score. He told me later, "I made you a hero in the Super Bowl" I said, "Thank you I appreciate

it." It's the end of my whole life. What I dreamed of as a boy was to play in the Super Bowl. To score a touchdown in the 20th Super Bowl—I'm overwhelmed by it. 1/27/86

Maybe we can make him president, too. 1/27/86

We'll keep using him and teams will keep saying "We can stop him," and they won't. 8/4/86

WEIGHING IN AT 350

It's not astronomical. Sometimes you can't keep those things under control. That's up to the individual, and the individual's wife, also. She cooks doesn't she? 12/27/86 Des Plaines Daily Herald

I just see a very, very, very short career if he doesn't change it. I worry about him five or six years down the line.
12/28/86 *Southtown Economist*

*If he doesn't take [the weight] off, he'll be in jeopardy of not being here, period. And I think I speak for the whole organization when I say that. I'm saying it'll be a different color jersey next year.
12/31/86* Chicago Sun Times

SAME OLD TUNE

Once again William Perry's weight was reported to be over 320. Ditka confirmed that Perry was now up to 333. Ditka had had enough and said for the first week, Perry would be fined $25 a pound. After that, the fines would double:
$400, $800, $1,600, $3,200, $6,400, $13,200 a pound. When it gets to that and he's not down to weight, you'll know he's silly. If he gets up to $5,000 a pound, he'll understand. 9/2/87 *Chicago Sun Times*

Maybe someone will ask him why his wife doesn't understand the importance of getting down. Let me get right to the heart of it. I think

somebody has to help him. I think she would be the most logical person to help him. I'm not evading the issue anymore. It's time to get down to what is important in his life. And I think that [his weight] is more important than a new gold chain. 9/2/87 Chicago Sun Times

William Perry:
I don't have any reaction to what Coach Ditka has to say. The only thing I'd like to say is just keep my wife out of it. It's between him and me. 9/3/87 *Chicago Sun Times*

He doesn't eat here [with the team]. He eats there [at home]. Or else between here and there. 9/2/87

William Perry:
We had an agreement I'd weigh 320 by the first game and that's what I'll be. Everybody goes up and down. 9/3/87 *Chicago Sun Times*

The Bears office staff received so many angry calls defending Perry's wife that Ditka commented:
We have women up there (answering calls in the office) wearing earplugs. I came in today and we had three people with swimming hats. 9/4/87 Chicago Sun Times

DITKA'S MESSAGE

I'll tell you something, William Perry is the furthest thing from my mind. I don't care if William Perry ever comes back. William Perry means nothing to me. We don't need William Perry that much. And if he comes back out of shape, he won't start. 10/6/87

You people think my life depends on William Perry. You guys are all wrong, man. His career depends on Mike Ditka a hell of a lot more than my career depends on him. You can book that.
10/6/87 Chicago Sun Times

THE TRUCE

After years of fighting William Perry's weight Ditka accepted the fact that William Perry's weight would always be higher than Ditka would like:
I look at the grades and the films, and as long as I and the defensive coaches are happy, I have no problem with it.
11/27/87 *Chicago Sun Times*

It doesn't do much good to rant and rave about it. It's too hard on me mentally and physically. I beat a dead horse to death before.
12/19/87 Chicago Sun-Times

William Perry:
As far as playing the run, I can do that with my eyes closed. That's why coach Ditka drafted me. 11/27/87 *Chicago Sun Times*

Sherry Perry, William Perry's wife:
The only thing I have to say is we don't put football first. Whatever Mike Ditka does is his right, but we put the Lord first and that's the way it's always been. We don't drill on football because football is just a game that comes and goes. We put our family and we put the Lord first. If you put football first in your life and then you're pulled off the field, you hurt. It doesn't affect either of us, because we know it's a game. We just need each other and our Bible... 12/30/87

After his return as a starter in 1989, after missing most of the 1988 season, Ditka noted:
I think his attitude is outstanding, but he has never had a bad attitude. The only time his attitude was even questionable was when he was injured and nonfunctional. I think that hurt him a lot. I don't think he felt comfortable being around here. Sometimes that's our fault. Maybe we don't make him feel as comfortable as we should. That's one thing bad about sports. When you're hurt, you're the outside guy looking in. It shouldn't be that way. But his attitude has been very good. He has tried very hard on the field. 10/6/89

Walter Payton

THE BEST FOOTBALL PLAYER EVER

I can't say enough about Walter Payton. Walter owes me nothing and he owes football nothing. He's given it all he has. 2/27/82

It's hard to compare. They're all unique. But Walter is the best because he's the most complete. He's the whole package. He may not do some things as well as someone else has done, but he does everything better than anyone else ever has. 9/2/84

I've not seen anyone approach him as a football player and he's probably the best athlete I've ever seen. 11/11/86

The very best football player I've ever seen, period. At any position. 11/5/85

CONTROVERSY: THE SUPER BOWL

More than anybody else's...this was Walter Payton's day. He deserves more credit for what happened than anybody else on the team. 1/27/86

Bear fans attending the Super Bowl game in New Orleans were chanting "Walter, Walter!" hoping that Walter Payton would get an opportunity to score in the 46-10 defeat of the Patriots. Walter never did. Ditka commented:
It's unfortunate Walter didn't get a touchdown, but Walter's contribution...nobody has to talk about it. The Patriots keyed their whole defense on him. 1/28/86

Walter Payton:
I was upset, a little hurt. Was. Not now. I got over it right away. You know how it is. You work all these years, you want to do well in

the big game, and then, something like that takes away from the moment. Maybe Mike Ditka got caught up in the game and didn't notice it. 1/30/86

BELIEVING IN EACH OTHER

People just believe in him. They know we have more than one way to get it done, and it's not necessarily the guy who takes the snap from the center. We rely on a lot of people in our offense, but nobody more than him. 1/2/87 Chicago Sun Times

Walter Payton:
He knows what it takes. He's been in this situation before. What he tries to instill in us is that we can only count on the team members. We can't believe things we read in the papers or what we hear on television. It's what you believe in your heart and what's on the team that counts. 10/21/85

**After meeting with Pete Rozelle on buying
a new football franchise, Payton commented:**
*If I get a team, Mike Ditka will be the coach.
5/13/87* Des Plaines Daily Herald

THE UNIQUENESS OF WALTER PAYTON

When you get older as a player, you can say, "Well, I don't have to work as hard." Or you can say, "I have to work twice as hard." And that's the way Dan [Hampton] and Walter look at it. I think Walter is working harder, but he's always worked hard. When you've accomplished what he has and then people in the media have the audacity to say we should do other things with other people... I just think he's going to shove that down people's throats. 8/7/87

Responding to people who want to see Payton used sparingly:
It's really interesting to see how soon people forget. I really think it's a great lesson to everybody in sports. Fame is fleeting. A lot of people

are very unappreciative about what it's all about. I'm not one of them. 10/30/87 Chicago Sun Times

When asked if he felt Walter Payton should have retired at the end of the 1986 season, Gayle Sayers responded:
No question. Mike [Ditka] is being so kind to Walter. Starting him, letting him play... Walter looks good, says he feels great. Still, it comes that time when you have to go out... He has nothing to be ashamed of. He has all the records you could want. He should say: "Lord, thank you very much. I enjoyed it. Goodbye."
12/3/87 *Chicago Sun Times*

Mike Ditka's reaction to Sayers' criticism of Walter Payton:
It's kind of ironic that Gale Sayers and Jim Brown would keep downplaying his [Payton] achievement. Regardless of how good runners they were, not either one of them could have carried his jock as a complete football player. Sayers was probably the most exciting runner ever to play the game. Brown was a great, great runner. But they didn't have the longevity. They didn't have the conditioning. They didn't have the heart. They didn't have the desire. They didn't have the records. They didn't have the blocking of Walter Payton. They didn't fake as good and they didn't catch as good. So it's kind of boring to keep letting those guys on television take shots at Walter. It's unfortunate they do that. They don't have to do that. Their place is assured. They're in the Hall of Fame. Payton will be there right next to them. I don't think it's something Payton would do, either. I don't think he'd criticize the next running back for Chicago. I think he'll compliment him. 12/3/87 Chicago Sun Times

I believe I was fortunate enough to deal with the best football player this league has ever seen, and he didn't bend rules. He abided by them. He was a great leader for them. Some of the other guys couldn't carry his jock strap and never will. They want to be catered to. They want to be individuals. They want to get away with not practicing. Here's the best who ever played the game, and if he's not good example for them, they must be blind. 2/8/88

PLAYER INTERACTION 1982-1992

THE ACQUISITION OF DOUG FLUTIE

There have been a lot of good football players at that position who weren't real tall. If a guy can do other things, you find a way to make sure he can throw the football. I just think he's a talent. I wouldn't have an interest in him at any other position besides quarterback. 10/3/86

After the Bears signed Doug Flutie in 1986, reporters challenged the logic for acquiring him. Ditka explained:
It goes back to what he accomplished in college. He did all that with players who are not household names in the NFL, so it must have been him. 10/15/86

Ditka comments on the acquisition of Doug Flutie and accusations of disloyalty to the back-up quarterbacks Fuller and Tomzak, particularly from Jim McMahon. Ditka shot back:
I haven't given up on anybody. I didn't bring him in to threaten anybody. We're going to take a look...see what happens. 10/16/86

Doug Flutie:
Ditka thinks I'm a winner. He has a lot of faith in me. I'm happy to have a chance to develop at my own pace. Look at John Elway. He had a terrible year as a rookie and this year he's been fantastic. But everyone knew he had great potential. If Doug Flutie had that kind of year as a rookie, all you would have heard is the "I told-you-so's. He's too short." 10/15/86

DOUG FLUTIE, BEAR QUARTERBACK

When President Kennedy won, they said he had charisma. This kid has character, charisma, and personality. And he works at it. I've been here five years and he's the only quarterback I've seen who is here early in the morning studying films and who comes back on Wednesday for the game plans early... I see Doug being an excellent, excellent quarterback in the NFL, period. 12/9/86

It's just like hollering at Bambi. I get letters from schoolteachers all over America telling me I'm not allowed to do that. So I probably won't do that anymore. 12/30/86

I did not misjudge Flutie. Maybe other people think I have within and without the organization. I did not misjudge Doug Flutie. I stand on that and back that... 4/29/87

TRADED

In 1987, the Bears announced that Flutie had been traded to New England for a future draft choice. He decided to cross the picket line and play for the non-union New England Patriots:
I firmly believe in the union and the things they are fighting for, but I saw this as a chance to get to New England and an opportunity that probably wouldn't have happened down the road.
10/14/87 Chicago Sun Times

Responding to reports that some Bears criticized Flutie for crossing the picket line to play for the Patriots. Ditka responds:
I've heard a lot of things. If the people who said them had half as much class as Doug they wouldn't have said those things. He's a classy young man. He'll do fine in life. I have great respect for him as a person. That's much more important than anything he'll ever do in football. I would have done nothing differently with Doug last year. It was a coaches decision; and I've always accepted that responsibility. I'm only disappointed he didn't lead the Bears to victory in the Super Bowl. I probably made a mistake going into camp this year. I kind of put Doug behind the 8-ball by not making him the starting quarter-back when camp opened. I don't know why I did that. But you don't tarnish quality. The trade wasn't even our idea. New England wanted him. 10/15/87

Trading Doug Flutie to New England seemed like admission that acquiring him had been a mistake. Ditka responded:
Who says it didn't work out? It doesn't take a Phi Beta Kappa to understand it was the best thing for Doug. And it's probably going to be a good thing for the New England Patriots. It remains to be seen how good a decision it is for the Bears. Contrary to what you experts think [the media], I haven't eaten crow or backed off one bit. I love Doug Flutie. I love what he stands for and how he plays. Hopefully, in his new situation, people will accept him the way he should be accepted. We made a decision based on what we felt was best for Doug and his situation. He wanted to play football. It didn't look like it was going to happen here." 10/15/87

Matt Suhey

Matt Suhey on Ditka:
He wants a standard and we have to live up to it. But if you go up and down the line there's no doubt the players respect Mike Ditka the man. 1/7/86

Suhey:
If you violate things that hurt the progress of the team, there's no question you won't stay in a Bear uniform long. He means what he says. It's not a mind game. He wants a dynasty attitude on the Bears. He wants it to be an attitude that's good for a number of years. 11/12/86

MIKE TOMCZAK

Ditka on Mike Tomczak:
Mike found out there are more important things in the world then women. Mike is a cute kid. If you're a nice-looking guy and you've some talent, you should be able to have some fun in your life. The thing I saw with Mike is that he worked on his mind. His take-charge ability's much better. I feel good with Mike in there. 8/23/87

Mike Tomczak on Ditka:
This year I have to play football. But I'm not the head coach. Sometimes he's not going to be happy and some-times I'm not. I'm not saying if I'd been in there we would have won the Washington game. Maybe it was some motivation to work harder. Because if that situation arises again, he won't have to second-guess himself or even think about putting someone else in. 8/16/87

Tomczak on the Bear quarterback situation:
You never know what's going to happen around here. Sometimes you get the starting nod and Jim comes out of the woodwork and says 'I'm ready to play.' I don't know if Coach Ditka will let that happen. He'll make his decision for the best of the team and I'll respect it either way. I'm not saying it's always fair, but he's been coaching a lot longer than I've been playing.
8/29/87 *Chicago Sun Times*

Ditka on the booing of Mike Tomczak:
I think [the booing] puts added pressure on him. He is trying to overcome. Therefore, you try to be a little more spectacular and that is what I don't want him to be. I want him to be good old-fashioned

Mike Tomczak, from the South Side of Chicago. A good Polish young man, and just play tough. Put his high-tops on and go to work.
1/2/91

After being traded to the Packers, Tomczak
reflected on playing for Mike Ditka:
I'm never going to remember him as a (jerk) or somebody I never got along with. I'll remember him as the one who told me, "You've got to play for pride and line up and do the best you can," that winning is great but the most important thing is giving it your all and the camaraderie you establish with all the guys in the league. That's what I carry from him. 11/27/92

DITKA ON JIM HARBAUGH

[Drafting Harbaugh] was a sound decision. Down the road he's going to be a very good player. 4/29/87 *Des Plaines Daily Herald*

On Harbaugh at mini-camp:
He looked doggone good—everybody looked good. Anyone who says he doesn't have a major-league arm is almost funny.
5/13/87 Des Plaines Daily Herald

In an intra-squad game, words were exchanged between
Harbaugh and Hampton and Dent. Harbaugh pushed
Dent in the face mask. Ditka was happy:
I like that in life. I'm not knocking anybody. I'm saying we're all on the same team for the same reasons, and if that guy can get us to the Super Bowl, I'd sure be on his side. I wouldn't be taking pot shots at him. Harbaugh doesn't pick up the papers every day and read how good these guys are. He's just trying to make a football team and be the best he can be. He forgot to read their press clippings. The Redskins [who beat the Bears in the 1986 playoffs] didn't read our press clippings, either... He has a dimension that's going to be tough to defense, because he's willing to run with it and he's smart. He didn't get out of Michigan because he's good-looking. He knows what he's doing. 8/10/87

Comparing Ditka to Bo Schembechler, Harbaugh commented:
When it comes to going after officials, Ditka is worse then Bo, except maybe when Bo was younger. He uses every word you can think of. At Denver last week, Ditka went after this one official and spit gum right in his ear. 11/23/87

In a Bear-Saint game in 1991, late in the 4th quarter, Harbaugh had only completed 2 of 19 passes. Ditka and Harbaugh discussed the situation on the sidelines:
Ditka: I'm going to take you out.
Harbaugh: Why?
Ditka: For a couple of reasons. I don't think you're doing that great. I think you're going to get killed out there.
Harbaugh: You can't take me out.
Ditka: I can take you out if I want to.
Harbaugh: Don't take me out. I'm going to win this game for you. I'll do something. I'm going to win this game for you.
Ditka: I don't know that you necessarily have to win it. Just don't lose it.
Harbaugh: OK, I won't lose it.
The Bears won 20-17 on a last minute touchdown pass from Harbaugh to Waddle. 10/29/91

Ditka on Harbaugh's last minute heroics:
He's amazing. There are very few guys who wouldn't have chucked in the towel. As a matter of fact, I was looking for a towel to chuck out there. It was tough on that guy. That's hard to do, boy. I have seen a lot of the great ones who would have said, "Hey, time out this is no fun." But he just did the best he could. 10/29/91

JAY HILGENBERG

Jay Hilgenberg on Mike Ditka:
The coaches and the organization have been behind me. They instilled the confidence in me. Ditka said opportunity doesn't come very often, so you've got to take it when you've got the chance. That's what we try to do. 1/13/86

Ditka after Jay Hilgenberg was traded to the Browns:

We miss him. And we appreciate all he did for the Chicago Bears. What's done is done. You can't undo it. He will go on and hopefully play well for them. And hopefully the people we have will go on and play well for us. 8/24/92

KEVIN BUTLER

I told you about Kevin Butler. He has the ability to be in the top one or two in the league. You gotta love him. Nothing bothers him. 10/14/85

He gets paid to kick the football, and if he doesn't kick it well enough, we have to find somebody else to kick it. 12/1/86

Butler's comments on what Ditka told him after his mistake in the Cleveland game:

You can't print what he had to say. 9/15/86

DITKA VS. RICHARD DENT

Ditka:

Where's Robert? I've got a game ball for him. 11/23/87

Dent:

The Coach's comments, they don't make me play any harder. Do I feel like I get the proper respect? If my mother wanted me to be Robert, then I wouldn't be Richard. 11/23/87

Dent:

I felt very embarrassed by being called out of my name. It was something negative on my mind. I don't care who I work for, I like to be respected. I know I'm a classy ballplayer and I like to be treated like one. Mike has to be able to get closer to his players. He has to find a better way of motivating his players... That's the only way to get the best out of everybody. 4/1/88 Chicago Sun-Times

MAURICE DOUGLASS

**Ditka was told that Maurice Douglass was
employed as a male stripper in the off-season:**
I thought he was a dancer, I didn't know he was...you know... Some's
got it, some don't. 8/5/87 *Chicago Sun Times*

He's more than a pretty face, gang. 11/23/87 Chicago Sun Times

MIKE SINGLETARY

He's a great example of what a football player should be. He works
harder than anyone we have on the team.   1/1/86

*Mike got up and was telling the defense what they had to do to stop
the Rams. By the time they were done, they had turned over tables
and chairs. 1/14/86*

Mike's case is very unique because he spent his whole career with
one team. He spent his career as an All-Pro, and he was the MVP as
a defensive player in the National Football League. And he is an
outstanding gentleman. He is an interesting guy. He is dedicated to
doing what is right and living his life in a certain way. You have got
to respect him for those things as much as anything. I would assume
that this is an agonizing year for Mike. He is going to put on the
uniform for the last year, and like a lot of us, he was expecting bigger
and better things. It just didn't happen. 12/13/92

OTIS WILSON VS. DITKA

**Ditka and Wilson exchanged words at halftime during the Bears
come-from-behind victory over the Chiefs. Wilson's view:**
*Mike said a few things that I didn't like and I said a few things he
didn't like. He told me to go home and I said, "I'll go home."*
11/5/87 Chicago Sun Times

Did Ditka mean he was finished forever? Otis said:
That's what he told me when I walked out the door. He said I'll never play anywhere else. *12/31/87*

Ditka's response:
He's a liar. 12/31/87

It's something that I think has blossomed into a misunderstanding. Hopefully we can get it straightened out tomorrow because he is a very important part of our football team. 12/31/87 Chicago Sun Times

DAN HAMPTON

Hampton explains dumping water on Ditka when the Bears clinched the Central Division championship in 1984:
Somebody had to show him [Ditka] the players were happy and joyous. I hope he took it as it was intended. We'll find out later. 11/26/88

Ditka's response:
The boys had their fun, they're entitled to it. 11/26/84

After Dan Hampton's ninth knee surgery, Ditka was asked what advice he would give to him:
It becomes very hard. And if it was, you know, a situation where it threatened the way he walked and his well-being for the rest of his life, then I would say get out of it anyway, period. That would be my advice. Nobody forces anybody in life to do anything. That's the tragedy. You play the game because you love it. Dan happens to be a guy that loves the game. So if you were to ask me what his decision is, he'll probably try it again. And in my case, I'd probably do the same thing. You play sometimes when you shouldn't. 11/1/89

Dan Hampton:
When you get right down to it, the guys who have made their mark on the game, Dick Butkus, Mike Ditka, Ed O'Bradovich...they don't walk away from the game, they limp away. 11/3/89

STEVE MCMICHAEL

...I'll tell you who's playing good. Steve McMichael. He just lines up and goes. He brings a lunch bucket and goes to work. Starts at noon, and he doesn't stop until the whistle goes. That's what it's all about. 10/1/85

Does McMichael have the ideal make-up for a football player? All depends what era you mean. Nineteen twenty-five he'd be right in there. He's a good ol' boy. 10/8/86

There is no point in being a nice guy out there. This is not a nice guy game. If it's a nice guy game, then millions of people could be doing this. It's a tough guy game. He is a tough guy and I think he provided a lot of leadership. 8/24/92

MCMICHAEL ON DITKA

Ditka is our constant. He keeps us together. People seem surprised by how he acts sometimes and I don't know why they are. I know how he'll react every time. Mellow coach means mellow players. I hope he keeps getting on our butts the same as always. He expects the best. I do, too. 10/8/86

You know, when I came here, we had some players who felt they didn't have to give it that extra effort. We had that kind of attitude in abundance. But Mike Ditka got rid of all of them. You can take all the geniuses with computers and chalk talks and films and stick it. You got to have people who want to play hard. It's Mike's team. It's Mike's baby. 10/14/85

I think I'm him reincarnated. Everything I stand for is his attitude. I am the same kind of football player he was. I love the guy.
10/28/87 Chicago Sun-Times

CHICAGO AND THE GRABOWSKIS

Winning and Losing in Chicago

On defeating the Redskins 23-19 in a 1984 playoff game:
It's time for Chicago to take a bow. 12/31/84

**The next week the Bears were shut out in the N.F.C.
title game by the San Francisco 49ers, 23-0:**
*We have no excuses. We were beaten soundly by a good football
team. I am disappointed for the players and for the fans in Chicago.
I apologize to the fans and the team. 1/7/85*

**Responding to statements that the Bears had replaced
the Dallas Cowboys as America's team:**
All we have to be is Chicago's Team. 11/17/85

**Before the 1985 N.F.C. championship game,
Ditka reflected on the Chicago jinx:**
*I realize people here had high expectations for the Sox and Cubs and
were disappointed. But I don't think you can compare different teams*

and different sports. If you can't get excited about the things in life that excite you, then something's wrong. Then do something else. If you're worried about hitting the ball in the water on the fifth hole, then don't play the fifth hole. 1/12/86

After the Super Bowl XX victory, Ditka scoffed at those who said Chicago Teams choked during big games:
Now they can't say that about us anymore or about any Chicago Team. Chicago has a winner. This victory today was a credit to the city of Chicago, and I hope the fans are loving it. We're supposed to be the city of big shoulders. Well, this is a team of big shoulders, a team that works together and gets a lot of things done. 1/27/86

I love to win. I love what it means to the city of Chicago and this organization. If anybody can't pay the price for that, we're in the wrong game. We ought to be delivering mail.
12/28/86 Southtown Economist

GRABOWSKIS

I don't think we come in favor with some people. There are teams that are fair-haired and some that aren't fair-haired. There are teams named Smith and some named Grabowski. We're Grabowskis. The Rams are a Smith team. 1/7/86

This [the NFC title game vs the Rams] is the Smiths against the Grabowskis. Chicago's been knocked too much. It's a great city, but it's been knocked too much. I'm happy we've meant something to the people here. I get letters, letters from wives. Wives thanking the Bears for making this winter so much fun. "My husband's never been in a better mood," one lady writes "because of your football team." People in Chicago, they've got passion. 1/12/86

John J. Kulczycki, professor, University of Illinois in Chicago:
[Grabowskis] don't wait for something to fall into [their] lap. This means a sustained pushing of the rock up the hill. 1/19/86

Jan Novak, Chicago novelist:
The Smiths are kind of reserved... We [Grabowskis] are the kind of people who yell and get angry and break our hands on lockers when we lose. 1/19/86

Ditka:
Let me tell you about these guys. We're down there [in Georgia prior to the Super Bowl] three days. We eat together, practice together, meet together, eat again together, then go to bed, and we wake up and look at each other again. I don't know if that makes you ornery or what, but these guys are ready. Not excited. Anxious maybe. They feel this is just part of the mission, this game here Sunday, no matter who we're playing or matter what the weather is...in other words, I like my Grabowskis. 1/12/86

We're appreciated in Brooklyn, Pittsburgh, Scranton, Wilkes-Barre, Birmingham, good work areas where people know what it's all about. We wouldn't fit too well in Beverly Hills, Miami, places like that. 1/26/86

AFTER WINNING THE SUPER BOWL

...my interpretation of Grabowski is he's the Crown Prince of Poland, he always dressed well. When we lose a couple, I'm sure you guys [the media] will have a ball with it. I can't remember a coach, when you look back at the 1960s, that didn't wear a coat and tie. 9/19/86

When asked if the Bears were still keeping the Grabowski image, Ditka said yes:
But the bowling shirts are going more toward Givenchy. 12/28/86

Being a Grabowski:
It reflects the work ethic, the great attitude, and that's what it is all about, it was the way I was raised. We said it was the attitude of the Bears, but it's the attitude of the city and of people who aren't afraid to work, who really live the American Dream, who are trying to get ahead. 7/16/87 *Chicago Sun Times*

**Reflecting upon signing his new contract and
making money outside of football in Chicago:**
*It's such a great city. It's provided me with opportunities kids don't
even dream about.* 8/30/87 Des Plaines Daily Herald

**When told that the "Grabowski Shuffle" video had sold 50,000
copies and qualified for a platinum award Ditka replied:**
It's an early Christmas present. I'm excited for the Grabowskis and
the fans, but I'll still be looking in my stocking for a Super Bowl
ring. 12/3/87 *Chicago Sun Times*

THE HATED PACKERS

Rivalry

It's hard for young kids to understand. They don't know. But they will know the first time somebody knocks them down when they are standing around on the field. They will know what it means. You try to tell them it has been a great rivalry for 70 years, but that doesn't mean they are going to get excited about it. But they had better pay attention, because if they don't somebody will take their head off. 10/20/92

I know at the time I played, it was probably the biggest game Mr. Halas ever prepared for. 11/5/89

Jerry Vainisi on Ditka and the Packers/Bears Rivalry:
I thought the rivalry had changed because the younger players on both teams don't remember the glory days. Maybe it picked up since Ditka has been coach. Since then, the spirit has been rekindled. Our players and [Packers Coach] Forrest Gregg's players have picked up on that. 9/22/86

Ditka on Packer spies:
In those days [1960s] there were spies around. We had people looking at the rooftops. Doug Atkins was always pointing to the pigeons. 10/21/85

They [Green Bay] are going to try to muscle you where they can, and we're just not a team that can be muscled very easily. We respond back to what they do, and they respond back to what we do. 9/18/84

The players would never mention the words "Green Bay" the week before a Packers Game. We were afraid the coaches might get all choked up. 10/21/85

When we play the Packers, you notice their players don't pick anybody off the ground and ours don't pick any of theirs up. 1/26/86

Ditka Declares War

It's not going to be like last year. We're not going to be the hittees. We're going to be the hitters. That's fact. 9/18/86

It will not be for the faint of heart. We'll play whatever has to be played to win the game. 9/22/86

It wouldn't have been as nice if we had blown them out... They [the Packers] just knew they were going to win the game. I think it hurts more when you squeak it by. 11/25/86

Charles Martin, Packer Lineman:
Coach Ditka called us a bunch of thugs. But we're just like his players. We're only human. Sometimes, we get a little physical, but it's a physical game. If you can't take it, it's not your game. 8/24/87

Forrest Gregg:
I know our games with the Bears the last couple of years have been pretty intense. That's just the way both of our teams play football. That's the way I played the game, and that's the way Mike Ditka

played it. I like Mike, regardless of what some people may think. We just compete. When we're at the league meetings, we converse. Believe it or not, we don't arm wrestle or hiss at each other. 9/13/87

Mike Ditka:
I think our guys are really looking forward to this game. Really looking forward to it. You can take that anyway you want.
11/3/87 Chicago Sun Times

Alphonso Carreker, Packer defensive end:
You're going to see some big plays and some big hits. I don't think the Packers have been dirty or committed any unsportmanlike fouls in the Bear games. Well maybe one or two. But other than that, it's usually the Bears. If they cheap shot someone, then it's OK. If another team does it to the Bears, it's looked at as a cheap shot
11/3/87 *Chicago Sun Times*

Rich Moran, Packer left guard:
From the first time I stepped onto the field against the Bears, it's been different than any other game. The intensity level, the way the coaching staff reacts to the Bears—it's just different.
11/3/87 Chicago Sun Times

MORE FUEL FOR THE FIRE

Jim McMahon:
I don't have much respect for Coach Gregg and I don't have much respect for some of their players. I think they used to have a real good organization. It just seems to me it's kind of gone downhill the last three or four years, and I think Forrest Gregg's got to be part of that. 11/3/87

Dave Duerson, after the Bears beat the
Packers 23-10 at Soldier Field:
We attempted to play this game clean. Mike Ditka has made it clear to us. He tells us every week we play the Packers that he's not going to have any cheap shots coming from us. If we start anything we're

going to get fined. And he means that. So we've played it within the rules. But we're concerned because we've lost a number of players in the Bear-Packer rivalry. Not because of great defense or great hits, but because of cheap plays. 11/30/87

I told my younger players that if they could imagine the greatest rivalry they had in high school or in college, this is a greater one, that's all. 9/16/90

It's probably the best rivalry in football. A lot of people have newer rivalries, but this thing has transcended a lot of years. There have been some heated games, but most of the games have been out of great respect for both organizations. There were probably a few years when things weren't played so smooth, but it has been pretty good football. 9/16/90

Why Bear players referred the Packers in the Lombardi era as the Red Bay Packers:
Because every time we said Green Bay, our coaches choked. 12/15/91

All you're going to get in a Packers-Bears football game is a good, tough football game. As long as you play within the rules of the game, it shouldn't bother anybody. It doesn't bother me and it shouldn't bother anybody else. 9/22/88

Ditka when asked about Packer head coach Forrest Gregg's reputed dislike for him:
Maybe I'm wrong, but I've always fashioned myself as a pretty likable guy. 9/22/88

DITKA FROM THOSE WHO KNOW HIM

MIKE DITKA'S WIFE, DIANA

I don't think he is an underdog. He is very confident in everything he does. But maybe he's trying to prove things to himself. 11/17/85

On meeting Mike Ditka for the first time:
He asked me to go to lunch and my mother always told me: Never pass up a free meal. Then we went to dinner and things went from there. I used to tell people he was a tight ass with the Dallas Cowboys. I didn't know what a tight end was back then.
5/18/97 *New Orleans Times-Picayune*

Diana Ditka:
When you're losing everybody in the whole city feels it. And believe me, my husband felt it more than anyone else.
5/18/97 New Orleans Times-Picayune

Diana Ditka on how Mike Ditka takes a loss:
He comes home and kisses the dog and kicks me. No, actually, he doesn't bring it home with him.
5/18/97 *New Orleans Times-Picayune*

MIKE DITKA'S DAD

I'll tell you something. I've seen him when he was very pleasant company. You couldn't ask for better. I've seen him when things weren't going right and I'll tell you what, he wasn't fit to talk to. 11/17/85

FORMER BEAR PLAYERS

George Blanda, quarterback, 1949-1958:

I'm just so pleased. I've always been a Mike Ditka fan. I'm so happy he has made believers where some of them were skeptical four years ago. I think the Bears are going to be good for a longtime. 11/10/85

Dick Butkus, linebacker, 1965-1973:

I remember when I first came to the Bears in 1965, and we're playing the Rams, I think, at some place in Tennessee, I think. It's only an exhibition game, but here he is, standing by the doorway to the field, yelling it up. He's never changed, and it looks like all these guys [The Bears] have that feeling now. 12/24/85

Bronko Nagurski, fullback, 1930-1939:

It took Mike Ditka a long time to get there and get straightened out. He was his own worst enemy for a couple of years. He's gotten himself straightened out and he's doing a good job now. 11/10/85

George Conner, tackle-linebacker, 1948-1955:

A lot of people thought the old man was senile when he named Buddy Ryan and Mike Ditka. But Halas wanted to give back something to the Bears and the fans and he gave them Ditka. 11/10/85

FAMOUS NFL PLAYERS

John Mackey, ex-Baltimore Colt tight end:

My idol was Mike Ditka. I used to study the way he did things. Ditka gave this one guy a physical beating like I've never seen before.

He was all over the field. From that day on, I wanted to be just like him. Ditka had a mean streak in him. He didn't accept punishment, he dished it out. 9/8/85

Roger Staubach, ex-Dallas Cowboy quarterback:
Mike Ditka is a fantastic coach. Mike wants to win very badly. Mike will not let anything come between winning. Hopefully he can bring that focus back. 2/10/87

Bob Griese, ex-Miami Dolphins quarterback:
I read the papers and I'm amazed at some of the things that are said. My relationship with Don Shula was a very close one, to the point where if I didn't like plays from the game plan, we wouldn't run them. From what I read, it's 180 degrees different in Chicago. Words back and forth, "I don't care what he thinks. I'm going to do this." I don't know. Maybe it works better that way. And Chicago has always been a little different anyway. 11/14/86

John Brodie, ex-San Francisco 49ers quarterback:
The only one thing you have to know about Ditka--that he'd just as soon knock your head off as look at you, the old man (Halas) ought to like that. 11/27/84

THE DALLAS ORGANIZATION

Tom Landry:
When he started with us, I didn't think Mike had the poise and all that was necessary to be a head coach. But he has matured greatly through the years. When he left, I was confident he would be successful. He wanted to coach the Bears so bad. 11/14/85

Jim Myers, former Ditka coach at Dallas:
No doubt about it, Mike is a rough-tough guy who identifies with the character of the Chicago Bears. And I think he'll transmit that to the players. Mike wouldn't go for a drinking, brawling team today. He's picked up a lot of Polish from the Cowboys... Mike will be tough. He'll demand conditioning and discipline. But he'll also recognize

the sophistication of the modern player. And he does know football.
The important thing is, he'll be going where he thinks he belongs.
1/24/82

DAN REEVES ON DITKA

Dan Reeves, former teammate of Ditka's and
NFL head coach of the Atlanta Falcons:
We hit it off right away. I had a picture of him in my mind but the picture was totally different when I got to know him. He's extremely competitive. If he gets beat, he doesn't want to quit. There are no gray areas for Mike. Either a guy's a player or he's not. Mike is always going to look for the guy who's highly aggressive. He's never cared about what a guy ran [in the 40] or how big he is. Mike makes people play hard, or he'll get somebody else. 1/22/86

On Ditka losing a card game to him:
He picked up his chair and threw it. All four legs stuck in the wall. I said, "Man, this guy hates to lose." 11/17/85

COACHES AND OTHER FAMOUS SPORTS FIGURES

Bill Parcells, NFL Head Coach:
Mike and I are similar in what we believe it takes to win football games. It's hard work. Play tough, and make the other guy know that you're there. 1/3/86

Jerry Glanville, former NFL Head Coach:
It's a credit to Ditka that they keep growing in their attack. It's all there; the number of different runs, formations, motion, shifting. Everybody would like to be able to do that. 12/21/86

Abe Gibron, former Bears and Buccaneers Head Coach:
The Bears reflect the way Mike played and the way Halas coached. We tried to do that; but we didn't have the personnel. The Bears take no prisoners. 11/10/85

Weeb Eubank, ex-Coach, New York Jets and Baltimore Colts:
I don't expect the Bears to play with the same intensity for the next two or three years. Things will happen that Ditka, or anybody else, won't be able to handle. It's human nature. 8/25/86

Yankee great Moose Skowron:
He played tough, he coaches tough, and he's always his own man. He reminds me a lot of Casey Stengel. I tell people Mike coaches like Casey managed. Casey would get on your butt real good when you screwed up. Get in your ear and scream. Mike does the same thing. I say, if you're a competitor who wants to win, you should want to get screamed at. When the screaming stops, that's when you're in trouble. I know I liked it when Casey yelled at me. Which was pretty much every day. 8/22/97 New Orleans Times-Picayune

George Steinbrenner, New York Yankee owner, on Ditka being tough with his players:
They might cuss and moan, but they want discipline. That's why Ditka is a winner. To me, he exemplifies all the things I think are great. I could take Mike Ditka and put him into baseball and win the World Series with him. 2/29/87

John Madden, former Raiders head coach:
The best thing a coach can do is be consistent. You can copy ideas, but not personalities. Mike Ditka, for example. Mike Ditka gets on his players, and people wonder how his players take it. It's his consistency. He does it to everyone. That's him. That's what Mike Ditka is. And that's the thing. You have to be who you are, what you are, all the time. Dick Vermeil. He was the same all the time. The ones you worry about are the ones who don't talk to players one week, then want to be their friends the next week. Then the players don't know who they are. 1/8/88

Jerry Burns, former head coach of the Minnesota Vikings:
He is a good guy, and I wish every coach in the league was of the same caliber. When he is on TV, I like to watch him on the sidelines. You know, he's spitting and chewing and what not. He looks like

Jack Nicholson, you know, the movie star...the guy who played in 'One Flew over the Cuckoo's Nest.' I love the guy. It gives you guys [the media] a lot of stuff to write about. All of that ends up here in our paper [in Minnesota]. But nobody takes him seriously. What the hell did he have in [the paper] today? "Frozen snot and blood coagulating before it hit the ground." I don't know where he is getting all that stuff. But it's copy. 11/8/91

More Burns on Ditka:
He babbles on about this, or he babbles on about that, particularly to the delight of the Chicago media, and they write about it. That reminds me that he is the Muhammad Ali of pro football. 11/8/91

Bear offensive coach Greg Landry:
When you see Mike and he is verbalizing, sometimes it is not that he is hollering at that individual. He might be explaining something different. People look at him and he is hollering at somebody and they say, 'Boy, he is chewing that guy out.' He might not be. He is just being very vociferous, but he is trying to make a point about somebody who made a mistake. 12/18/91

Jimmy Johnson, NFL Head Coach on Ditka:
I know Mike is a great coach and motivator, and I have a tremendous respect for him. I have had a chance to visit with him a little over the last few years. He's one of the special coaches... 12/27/92

FORMER PLAYERS

Jim Harbaugh, former Bear quarterback:
I was in my second year (1988) and it was a preseason game. I was playing in the second half, and I scrambled for about 15 yards. Then I just lost the ball, kicking it off my thigh. I came to the sideline, and I didn't know what Ditka was going to say to me. He came over to me—I'll never forget it—he said, "Son, I don't care what round you were drafted in. I don't care what you did in college. You've got to produce at this level." I was kind of there just going along, making good money. The next game was against the Raiders, and I knew I

had to have a good game. I was nervous about making the team, especially when the coach tells you that you had to produce. The next game I had a hell of a game. I knew then that this game was about production, what you did on the field. I knew from that point on the mental toughness that I would need to acquire to play for the Bears, to play for Ditka and to play in the National Football League. I credit Mike Ditka for giving me that mental toughness that I needed. 8/24/97 New Orleans Times-Picayune

Mike Singletary, former Bears linebacker:

All great coaches make mistakes. Sometimes you want things so bad that you forget some of the little things that it took to climb the mountain...But overall, I think the layoff was good for him. It gave him time to reflect and see how much he missed the game. I think he'll come back swinging. 8/24/97 *New Orleans Times-Picayune*

Vestee Jackson, who played for Don Shula and Mike Ditka, on the difference between them:

Mike Ditka gives players more freedom, more of a chance to be themselves. You can be more of an individual as a Bear. Here, [in Miami] they coach 'team.' Coach Shula doesn't let you be much of an individual... I really don't like it, but coach Shula has won a lot of games doing it the old-fashioned way. It just seems like Mike Ditka gives guys a little more freedom to be a man and to take responsibility for your actions. 11/25/91

DA BEARS, DA BULLS

Chicago Bulls basketball coach Phil Jackson:

He doesn't face the same press I do or the same market that I do. But I know he's had a lot of support in this town, and it's very easy after a couple of years for that support to wane. And whatever you have done well, people start to take for granted or find holes in it. I'm envious of his strength in the city and the fact that he's had some great success and support here from the fans. I hope I can do as well for as long as he has. 10/23/92

**Mike Ditka on Phil Jackson, after Jackson signed
a $5.7 million contract to coach the Bulls in 1997:**
*More power to him. By God, he deserves it. Every dollar. Just look
at what the man has done. Sure the Bulls have Michael [Jordan].
But two teams have had Shaquille O'Neal. And how close have they
come to winning championships?*
7/25/97 New Orleans Times-Picayune

Bears defensive end Alonzo Spellman:
His name[Ditka's] is just as big as Michael Jordan's in Chicago... I
can't explain how much I respect him or how good it is to see him
back in the game doing what he loves to do. I expect him to do well
this year. 8/22/97 *New Orleans Times-Picayune*

Chicago columnist, Bill Gleason:
*You have to understand, Mike Ditka remains a dominant personality
because he's so Chicago. He has a toughness that fits the city's
steelworker mentality, if you know what I mean. Chicago has a way
of falling in love with personalities who are larger than life. Abe
Gibron, who used to coach the Bears, was like that. They loved Abe,
even though Abe didn't win. Mike won. Mike was the same kind of
player in college he was as a pro. So Chicago knew all about him by
the time he got to the Bears. This week [prior to a Bears-Saints
preseason game] they've been showing, over and over, one of his
great moments as a Bear, when he caught a pass and created a pinball
effect, with tacklers bouncing off him as he went down the field.*
8/22/97 New Orleans Times-Picayune

DITKA AND THE MEDIA

On press questions before the Super Bowl:
We have no control over the types of questions. By the time it's over, they have written everything you do from Grade 1 to 12 and that you probably stole a car in high school. 1/16/86

A LITTLE ANIMOSITY?

You're the same people who tell Spud Webb he can't play basketball and Wally Backman he can't play second base and Len Dykstra he can't hit a home run. We also have a quarterback who is 6 foot with a bad eye. You guys think you can't come out of the ghetto and be president. That's what you guys think. But Flutie isn't asking anybody to put him on stilts. 10/23/86

You guys keep on telling them [the Bears] they're good. Don't do that. You say negative things about me. You can find negative things about them and use them. 10/14/86

97

I don't want to say too much now because last week you got a couple geniuses in the media in Chicago. They were offended when I said we didn't play good last week. I only speak the truth. I don't bullcrap people. Today we played great. We just got a couple of bad breaks. If that's what you want to hear, you're talking to the wrong person. You're dealing in fiction. I don't deal in fiction. I deal in reality. I've been around the game 25-26 years and I know what good and bad is. I know what execution is, and I know what lack of execution is. And I don't need anybody in the media to tell me what it is. 10/20/86

Holding up a newspaper at a press conference:
See this. I read about him [Flutie] in the newspaper. I believe everything I read in the newspaper. No, I just liked everything I'd seen about him and everything I'd heard about him, characterwise. And then, I guess, when people tell me that he's not the answer, then I think more he is the answer. 12/28/86

DISH IT OUT, MIKE

Jim [McMahon] and I have a mutual admiration society. Now how are you going to headline that one? 8/14/86

At the start of a local post-practice press conference, to a TV cameraman:
Give me a break on those lights. I had a pimple and it was showing the other day. 10/1/87 *Chicago Sun Times*

Ditka's response to one reporter who repeatedly asked about the Fridge's weight:
You're the only overweight guy in this room and you keep asking about Perry's weight. 8/2/87 Southtown Economist

An old friend sent an essay he wrote about Ditka years ago in college. Teased Ditka:
He wrote an essay on me 30 years ago when he was a freshman at New Mexico. I had never seen it. He got an A on it. If you guys are

good, I'll let you have the essay. You'll sell a lot of papers. It's a true story. What life is all about. You start at the bottom and work your way to the top. Even though it refers to me, I forgot about it. I forgot about those days 30 years ago. It's interesting. 11/22/87

Earlier in the week Ditka said that the Bear defense stunk. After beating the Lions, reporters asked if the Bear players responded to his criticism of the defense. Ditka's reply:
I don't know. You guys responded. You all wrote it. That's all that counts. You guys have no imagination. I have to tell you what to write and then you write it. 11/23/87

I'm going to say one thing to you people. We average how many plays a game? Would you guess 64 or 65? In six games, what does that come out to be? About 400. On 399 of the plays I have been calm. And on one I have been excited. Yet you sons of bitches made a big deal out of it. That's life. Remember that. One out of 400 I got excited this whole year. One. As long as you remember that, don't ever ask me another question about those things. Because I won't answer it and I will walk out of here. You want to talk about football, fine. If you don't then go somewhere else. Anyone of you. All of you. You want to write about it, you go somewhere else. You want to talk about football, you talk about it. If you think this is a soap opera, you're [crazy]. Now, what else do you want to know? 10/20/92

GENIUSES

After the play-off loss to the Redskins, the media played up the idea that major changes next season were certain:
You're making like we have to clean house here. We have to make a few changes, not wholesale changes. There's no need for that, despite what you experts write and broadcast. You geniuses. 1/12/88

On some of the media and players criticizing Bears playcalling:
[Have the media call] the first play of each quarter and have the players call the rest of them. 1/12/88

There's a lot of ways you analyze. But until you know what you're talking about, players and media should keep their mouth shut. 1/12/88

MIKE DITKA: MEDIA SENSATION

Fred Danzig, editor of Advertising Age:
To get a guy who stands in such a demonstrable way for not tolerating less than the best is something almost any company would like. 1/8/89

Al Golin, president of Golin Harris, a Chicago-based public relations company:
Mike seems to be something for every man. While everyone seems to couch responses and comments in diplomatic terms, Mike seems to break through those kinds of rules and cut through the nonsense. He appeals to the Joe Six-pack type as well as executives. To Joe Six-pack, he is the guy from the neighborhood who made good. To the more educated and sophisticated, he seems to bring the order and regimentation they agree is necessary in running a business and in raising children. 1/8/89

To the Chicago media:
We're gonna throw deep for you, and you, and you and you. We're gonna be airing it out. You won't believe it. 8/16/91

THE LOUSY PEOPLE IN THE MEDIA

After a three-game losing streak:
The only thing that this losing streak is doing is that it has made a lot of people happy in the media. People at the [Chicago]Tribune, who own [radio and TV stations] WGN. People at the [Chicago] Sun-Times, who pay the jerks that write for them. And people at some of the radio and TV stations. That's my feeling exactly. At least we have made somebody happy. That's the malcontents and the lousy people in the media. 11/17/92

On firing back at radio callers who criticized him and his point of view:

[To] stick my head in the mud and not answer people when what they say is totally wrong would be contrary to what I believe. 12/3/92

All I can say is I know who I am and what I am and what I stand for. Nobody else can write about that and tell me who I am. And I'm going to be judged not by the people in this room [members of the media], God forbid. I'll be judged by my Creator, period. When all is said and done, perfection was never something that I espoused to... I never espoused to be perfect. I espoused to be the best me I can be. For 52 years I made a hell of a run at it. Just check the past record and I'll stand on it. 9/3/92

Responding to a book that was critical of Ditka:

I learned a long time ago that life was going to go on. When I'm gone, there's going to be a small ripple and it's going to continue right on. It happens, you know. There's just more important things than dragging up what happened 20 years ago or 10 years ago or five years ago. It's not significant on our society and it's not significant in my life. 9/3/92

I don't anticipate doing a radio show next year. It certainly hasn't evolved the way I anticipated. There have been a lot of things that have become disappointing to me. But I am a big boy. The heat in the kitchen never bothered me. 12/3/92

In a response to a Chicago sports writer identified by the Chicago Tribune as "apparently Bernie Lincicome:"

It seems it doesn't matter if you win or you lose in this town. To me, we will just go out and play 'em and you write what you want to write or say what you want to say. If you try to be honest with people, they don't appreciate it because they're jerks. Never in my life have I seen a bigger jerk than the one guy in this city. I mean that's appalling that a newspaper would hire a guy to do what he does. Because there is no good in life. Good is death. Good is disease. Good is plague. Good is communism. To him. So if that's what it is, fine. But why pull a hoax on the American public, or the public of Chicago. It's interesting, that's all. And I mean that from the bottom of my heart... Hemingway had talent. This man has no talent. Hemingway had guts. This man has no guts. I still believe talent means nothing if you don't have the heart for it anyway. What I'm trying to say is, that's what I believe. I will never back off what I believe. 9/3/91

You don't have fun when you're getting beat; nobody does. That's just part of the game. If you [the media] expect me to be laughing and having fun when I'm getting beat, you're crazy. 11/5/92

Joe Mooshil an Associated Press reporter:
Ditka's great. He's great copy. Whether he puts you down or whatever, he'll be a good story. 11/30/89

Sometimes I think the reporters don't know what the hell they're talking about and I think, 'What right do they have to ask that question?' But I do think a lot do know a lot about it and should straight from the shoulder. 11/30/89

Addressing the Chicago media's negativism:
You see the sarcasm. You see the things that are positive as negative. You see things I say that are negative, as positive. So you see what you want to see. That's embarrassing because I think that you have an obligation to report the truth. 9/6/88

After criticism in the media that the Bears were in transition:
Those of you who construe that as being negative, you're fools. That has nothing to do with negatives. It's got to do with reality. We live in a reality world... We're turning people over, trying to make our football team younger and replacing people who are getting older and still play good football. But one of the [media] geniuses saw it as a negative. 9/6/88

THE NEW ORLEANS MEDIA

You people say, "Are people tight out there? Are you pressing to stay away from them? Is that what's making you fall into them." I don't know. This is uncharted territory for me. I've never been there before. I don't know what's going on. I mean 19 turnovers in three weeks, I've never heard of it.
9/17/97 New Orleans Times Picayune

Jim Gallagher, sports director at WVUM-TV, New Orleans:
Mike is more professional than [former Saints coach, Jim] Mora was to deal with. Ditka understands the needs of TV and reporters. 9/28/97 New Orleans Times-Picayune

After the Saints victory over the Bears, 20-17, with Shuler going 9 for 23 with one touchdown and one interception, Ditka sent a message to Shuler and the New Orleans media:
Every day is important for him. I'm not issuing ultimatums. What you guys [the media] don't understand, see, is...I would not assume that you think I think you're my friend. And I know better. You're not. ...You people are all vultures, in my opinion. And I only say that in a complimentary way. But you will pluck the flesh the first chance you get. So if I make the decision to change him, then the article will be, or the comments will be, "pulled the plug too quick." And if I don't, then you'll write something else. But that's your opinion. I'm not in this for a popularity contest. Because I could care less what you think. But I'll make that decision. And when I make it, it's only made for one thing—for the best interest of this football team. 10/6/97 *New Orleans Times-Picayune*

Greg Suit, Saints senior vice president of marketing and administration:
Mike is such a good communicator. He really understands that when he's talking to the media, that he's also talking through the media to the fans. 10/17/97 New Orleans Times-Picayune

Ditka about being in a 1997 Saturday Night Live skit:
I played the part of the media. It was very hard to act intelligent. I was trying, but it was very hard to get anything out that made sense. I had a job as a writer with the Times-Picayune.
10/25/97 *New Orleans Times-Picayune*

Who cares about last week and me? You people make a big deal about me. It's not me; it's the players. It's about this football team. You guys want to make a big deal about my personality. You either like it or you don't like it. If you don't like it, you sure write about it enough. 12/2/97 New Orleans Times-Picayune

WINNING AND LOSING 1982-1985

1982 Mike Ditka: Rookie Head Coach

I told them [the players] there's no difference between them and the players in Dallas or San Francisco. It's all in the head. I told them who I am, just a guy going through life who was given a job I love. If they're as proud to be associated with the Bears as I am, we'll have no problems. 4/3/82

I just told them they are going to run more than ever. They're [the players] going to be in better shape and they're going to appreciate it more than ever. They're going to be in better shape, and I hope it's the winning edge. 4/3/82

Everybody has been told they are going to run. Some say there's nowhere to run in Chicago in the winter. There's lots of places to run. They can run in the hallway here [at Halas Hall] for 30 yards. I expect some players will say I've always done it some other way. I'll say, "Yeah, what did it get you?" 4/1/82

THE BEARS REACT

Jim Osborne:
I think he felt he had to make an impression on us to show us that he did have a plan to make us a winner. 8/8/82

Mike Singletary:
Some of us haven't been this small since high school. 8/8/82

Gary Fencik:
I don't think any of us knew we were going to have a physical camp as this, but we were under no delusions that it was going to be easy. 8/8/82

Doug Plank:
The ship is going to be run a little differently. Before it was left up more to the individual to work out. Now it's more programmed. And Mike said we're going to be together more as a team. 4/3/82

AFTER THE FIRST CAMP

Anybody who doesn't come to camp is foolish. There's an old saying, "Out of sight, out of mind." You can only evaluate what you see. 7/12/85

Ditka decided that the Bear camp location in Lake Forest, a suburb of Chicago should be moved. He compared Lake Forest to the old Bears camps in Rensselaer, Indiana:
Guys I didn't socialize with or know real well I got to know much better. When you went down to the corner tap and had a couple of beers after working out for 6 hours in 90 degree heat, the camaraderie became much greater. In Lake Forest everything is very cliquish. I'd like to see us do things as a team, totally. 7/15/84

If we approached it like a war, it would probably be better for us. We'd have fewer guys patting each other on the fanny all the time. 7/15/84

You can fool yourself about football. Basically, it is blocking and tackling. We wanted to find out some things early. Most players look forward to hitting and the ones who don't, that's what you want to find out. 7/27/82

THE DRAFT

Draft strategy—selecting the best athlete available:
That's always worked for the Cowboys so I don't see why it wouldn't work for the Bears. 1/21/82

The draft never was my bag entirely. It never is the head coach's bag entirely. Anyone who says it is, is foolish. I have to depend upon my scouts, the general manager, the president, and Bill Tobin, our scouting director. 11/12/83

I think you win on defense. I don't think that ever changes. You have to keep your defense strong and you don't want to get into the position where you have to turn three or four people over in one year, I don't want to do that. 4/26/87 Des Plaines Daily Herald

You've got to keep a certain number of rookies every year. Good teams find a way of resupplying. If you have all the experience in the world and line up against somebody with more physical ability, you'll get beat. 8/31/83

The Bears have now got a foundation they can build on for years and if they keep drafting as well as we've been fortunate enough to draft the last couple of years and not be afraid to play people, I think they have a chance to really do good things. 7/15/84

WIVES AT TRAINING CAMP

Commenting on Ditka's rule that wives are not allowed to stay in the area during training camp, Debra McMichael explained:
You know what [Ditka] ought to be thankful I keep [Steve] under control. If he was wild, he'd probably miss practice and get drunk

all the time. He ought to thank me for keeping him healthy.
12/15/87 Chicago Sun Times

Ditka's response:
Well, I disagree with Debra McMichael. Next year what we'll do if she wants to come to training camp is just let Steve stay [in Chicago] with her. That's why you have training camp.
12/15/87 Chicago Sun Times

Steve McMichael:
During the day, I'm concentrating on football, but at night I want to have somebody there to tell my problems to—and that's not some girl in a bar. 12/15/87 Chicago Sun Times

1982: The Season Begins

The pre-Mike Ditka Bears:
They didn't like losing, but it seemed to be a way of life, so they accepted it. You find ways to blow games. You find a way to blow a last-minute game in Minnesota just because those sons of guns have purple uniforms on. That's bull. I don't believe in that. 11/17/85

It's got to be a physical, intimidating football team. 1/24/82

After a 10-0 loss to New Orleans the day before the 1982 strike began:
We struck yesterday. If they strike, we're right in tune. We're a day ahead of schedule. 9/21/82

After the New Orleans loss, Ditka was particularly angry:
I believe some don't take it seriously enough, when you're supposed to pull on a run and you don't, or pull on a pass block and you don't get there on time, or you run the wrong pattern, your head isn't in the game. It takes total commitment. We have guys who haven't totally committed to what we're doing. 9/20/82

Robin Earl told reporters that after the New Orleans loss, Ditka said all players would have to re-apply for their jobs:
He said the door will be open and anybody who wants to play should see him. If anybody doesn't want to play or wants to be traded, he'll be willing to oblige. He said a few changes will be made.
9/20/82

After the Bears lost to Seattle 20-14 on a quick kick, which Ditka described as "a high school play," Seattle coach, Mike McCormack, took offense. Ditka's response:
I never said they were inferior. Basically what I said is we beat ourselves with bad field position, and I said the quick kick was a well-designed play. There's nothing wrong with high school plays. If Mike McCormack (Seattle Coach) finds that offensive, that's his business. I'm not going to worry about what anybody says. I said they aren't a great football team because they're not. 12/15/82

After his first season as Bear head coach, Ditka was optimistic:
It's like if you have a nice looking apple and you have a little bad spot, you have to peel it off. It's not a cancer that has to be removed, just a few blemishes we have to change around. 1/4/83

1983: Searching for a Way to Win

It's just a matter of some teams knowing how to win, some don't know how to win. We're going through that right now. We hope we are finding out how to win. Teams like Dallas and the Raiders know how to win. They find ways to win. They believe they can win. They never believe something's not going to happen. 10/14/83

As the Bears lost to the Detroit Lions 38-17 in a home game, an angry fan threw a drink at Ditka:
I had earphones on most of the time which is really maybe a godsend because I didn't hear what they were saying. I had a drink thrown, but if that's the worst thing that happens to me, I got it made.
11/1/83

**In the middle of the 1983 season the Bears owned a
dismal 2-5 record. As they embarked on their next game
in Philadelphia, Ditka took a hard line:**
I told them [the players], "Don't get on the plane if you don't want to
play." I didn't care if I went on the plane with 15 players. If you
don't want to bust your ass stay home. Get out of my sight. We won
7-6 and it wasn't pretty either. And we lost the next two games. But
I felt with the Philadelphia trip they started to understand what we
were trying to do here. 12/31/84

1984: Building a Winner

Ditka saw the 1984 season, his third with the Bears, as pivotal:
*The Bears have now got a foundation they can build on for years,
and if they keep drafting as well as we've been fortunate enough to
draft the last couple of years and not be afraid to play people, I think
they have a chance to do really good things. 7/10/84*

On November 25, 1984, the Bears defeated the Vikings 34-3 in
Minneapolis to win their first championship since 1963.
Characteristically, Ditka spoke of George Halas' confidence in him:
This is for the 49 guys in there [the locker room] and for the guy who
hired me (George Halas). Somewhere, he's smiling pretty good right
now. 11/26/84

*I hope the players see what I'm trying to instill here. When I came,
too many guys were in football just for a paycheck. You can't live
that way. I don't care if the players like me now. I just hope they
respect what I'm trying to do. I'm sure they still look at me sometimes
and think "Who is the jerk on the sidelines?" But, you know, football
isn't all X's and 0's. It's people. 12/4/84*

Our guys just don't take any crap. We don't like to be bullies, but we
don't like to be bullied either. 12/23/84

The Bears played their first play-off game in Washington, against the Redskins:

We have our work cut out for us. I don't think anybody understands what it's like to play in R.F.K. (Washington's Stadium). It's tough. They only get 52,000 people, but you got no friends. None. It's tough. We have to concentrate, play our game, forget the fans; don't play the scoreboard, play the opponent. If we can do that, we can be effective. 12/25/84

The Bears defeated the Redskins 23-19. The next Bear opponent was the San Francisco 49ers:

If I'm Montana [49er quarterback] watching today on TV, I gotta be prepared to throw that ball in a hurry. With our defense today, Joe Theismann, [the Redskins quarterback], he had to get rid of it in a second. They were fabulous. I'm not surprised... This is some football team here. 12/31/84

Ditka felt confident prior to the 49er game:

Nobody awes this football team, I still like our chances. 1/4/85

The thing that is in our favor is that even though they know more about our defense than they did a year ago, they've still got to defeat it. 1/6/85

The confident Bears lost to the 49ers 23-0 and were eliminated from the playoffs:

I apologize to our fans and to the team. We'll be back. The 49ers are a better football team than us right now. They just beat the butt off us, that's all. 1/7/85

At the end of the game, the 49ers placed a lineman in the backfield, further humiliating the Bears. Ditka was calm.

I've got to give them credit. How many guys would think of putting a guard in the backfield? Plus you got the best quarterback in football, and you put him out as a flanker. I think Bill [Walsh] was ready for this one. They taught us a lesson. 1/8/85

1985: Road to the Super Bowl

The most important thing for this team to realize is that what you do one year has nothing to do with what you'll do the next year. Everyone has a tendency to say, "Well, you were successful in '84 so therefore you automatically have to be successful in '85." That just does not hold water unless you are willing to pay the price. 7/21/85

We are not going to surprise anybody. Teams know the kind of football we are capable of. 9/4/85

We are not San Francisco, we are not San Diego. We are not Miami. We are the Bears. I like that. Being the Bears is not too bad. 9/4/85

If you can stay away from key injuries, you've got a chance, if you're a good football team. Our schedule is tough. Evidently we've got two good teams in our division [Minnesota and Detroit at the time 3-1 on the season]. We have a great rivalry with Green Bay. We play an excellent Miami team on the road, and an excellent San Francisco team on the road, and an excellent Dallas team on the road. The Jets look like they know what they're doing, and we've got them on the road. When you look at our schedule, that's why I say it's going to be tough. 10/6/85

Prior to a rematch with the 49ers in the 1985 season:
What if we both don't show up? They're the best team in football. Most intimidating defense I've ever seen. Most innovative offense that's ever been coached. 10/10/85

Not surprised at the 8-0 start:
I'm not saying that to be conceited or cocky or otherwise. I'm just not surprised because I'm not going to deal in negatives. If you had speculated before the year, it would be pretty far-fetched. But I think we've legitimately won them all. To go 16-0 would be a little far-fetched, also. But stranger things have happened. 10/28/85

If people want to say we play good offense because of McMahon and Walter Payton, that's fine. I don't care. If they say we play good on defense because it's Buddy's defense, that's okay. They're all working for the Bears. I don't want the credit, I just want the wins. 11/17/85

After the Bears only loss of the season to the Miami Dolphins:
We had a Bear football team and we lost that in the last few weeks. All of a sudden we just had a defense... Our Bear defense is perfect when the offense is capable of scoring and the special teams are capable of getting us field position. 12/4/85

1985 Play-off preferences
I have no preference at all. We've played hard enough and earned the right to get into the playoffs and play at home. Now whoever we have to play will have to come in here and it just doesn't matter. They're all good football teams. 12/22/85

Shortly before winning the Super Bowl:
We'll be the underdogs, no question about it. Maybe we're doing too many Super Bowl Shuffles... Say I'm concerned. Say I'm terrified. Anything you want... We couldn't beat a playoff team today. We would have been eliminated. 12/23/85

How to win the Super Bowl:
Put a chip on your shoulder in July and keep it there until January. 1/26/86

After the Bears defeated the New York Giants in the playoffs, Ditka looked forward to playing the Los Angeles Rams:
We're a better team than we were last year. Our determination has been good all year. If you have watched us play, we play hard. That's all you can ask. 1/12/86

There's a poem that says something about we've come many miles, but we've got many miles to go. I don't want to sound like I'm not happy about what happened today, but we're on a mission and it won't be finished until we're finished in New Orleans. 1/13/86

**Ditka feared that the Bears might be
too happy going to the Super Bowl:**
That's the worst thing you can be, a lot of teams are happy to be
there the first time they go. You can't go that way. 1/14/86

Super Bowl!

Dan Hampton:
*He told us to have fun. We shouldn't try to inhibit ourselves. The
media has a job to do. It only becomes a distraction if we make it a
distraction. 1/21/86*

When you get this far [to the Super Bowl] if you can't concentrate
on football, you better get another job. We're just going down to
play a game. The Patriots will go down and do the same thing.
Everybody will enjoy it, and then we'll go on with our lives.
1/16/86

*It's not life or death. It's not going to be World War III. But it will be
interesting. 1/19/86*

**Ditka reflecting on the Super Bowl
victory to a Chicago reporter in 1997:**
I don't care if they [the Bulls] win nine NBA titles. The '86 Super
Bowl was the greatest thing to happen to Chicago sports. That's the
way I feel... People loved that team, those guys, the attitude of those
players. They adopted them. Those guys went out and played their
[butts] off. They hit, they had personality, they had fun. They didn't
make it drudgery. People could relate to them because they were
doing what they did as kids—going out, having fun, beating up on
people. That's what they liked about it. That team epitomized that
city, the city of big shoulders. That's what that team was.
8/18/97 *Chicago Sun-Times*

LOSING THE EDGE 1986-1987

1986: The Bears Are No Longer Invincible

I get a little madder [at the 1986 Bears] because we're the world champions and I feel we shouldn't do wrong things, which is a foolish thought. I doubt that it's right, but I doubt I'm going to change. 10/11/86

I'm a little crabbier this year, and I don't smile as much. I dress a little better, but that's about it.   10/11/86

....you don't know Mike Ditka if you think success will spoil him. I've been so fortunate. Bud Grant said when I was hired it was not what you know but who you know. I'm just glad coach Halas knew me. 1/28/86

I'm not being bothered by anything the rest of the year [1986], as you'll find out. No more pressure. Pressure's over. I don't worry. 11/2/86

Having fun in the '86 Season?

I really am. It's been a struggle this year, but a fun kind of struggle. It's still serious business to me because it's my job and I want to win as much as I can. But I'm having fun. I don't think I've been uptight. I get ticked off on the sidelines. But off the field, I haven't exploded. 12/28/86

It became a little strained at times, and that I don't like. I really feel when it's drudgery to come here in the morning I wonder. Because I know if we had to go out and work in the mill like my Dad did, that was work. This is not work. 1/5/87 *Des Plaines Daily Herald*

I took a more businesslike approach and maybe the players took a more businesslike approach, and it wasn't as much fun. 1/5/87 Des Plaines Daily Herald

I guess the major difference in me is that I've learned not to take things so personally. We've come a long way from that first year, but we've come it together. 1/7/86

It's funny to me, it's still a game. Most of us coaches are overpaid as it is. 1/2/87 Chicago Sun Times

Would Ditka own an NFL Team?

That would be something I would seriously contemplate. There's a lot of ways you can leave a mark in football and society. Coaching is only one of them. Ownership, part of front-office management, I just think there's different ways, and I think somewhere in life you start thinking about them. Not right now, but someday. 1/2/87 *Chicago Sun Times*

During the 1986 season the Bears seemed distracted by the events surrounding the acquisition of Doug Flutie and Jim McMahon's criticism that the Bear organization was disloyal to the backup quarterbacks Mike Tomzak and Steve Fuller:

I didn't see us playing as a team Sunday. We didn't pick up one another as well as we had to. I don't know if was caused by last

week's sequence of events or not. I don't have all the answers. I'll listen to anyone, coaches or players, anyone who has a helpful suggestion to make. 10/21/86

We are no longer head and shoulders above anybody. 11/5/86

I don't think anybody ever thought we were invincible because we're not. Last year we played hard and won a lot of games. Now we're playing hard and we've lost a couple. I don't know if that's the invincibility factor. I know if I played on another team against the Bears, I wouldn't think they were invincible. I never thought the 49ers were, the Raiders, the Redskins. Other teams that play us love royally to kick our butts. That's a fact. Period. 11/5/86

With the loss of Jim McMahon, Ditka rallied the Bears around the notion that no one was indispensable:
One person didn't make us Super Bowl champs. We can overcome anything. 11/30/86

Ditka on Bears critics pointing to an easy schedule during the season as an obstacle to winning Super Bowl XXI:
You go tell our opponents that we have an easy schedule. They're ready to play us. Tell Green Bay, Pittsburgh or any of those clubs they aren't a lot of competition. It's been a dogfight all year. 1/3/87 *Des Plaines Daily Herald*

LOSING THE FIRST PLAYOFF GAME

The Bears lost their first playoff game to the Washington Redskins 27-13 at Soldier Field. Ditka tried to downplay the disappointment:
You can't take away what we did. We lost the battle, but we didn't lose the war. We're still a young team and still learning. Maybe we're learning as coaches, too. I was confident we'd win the game, but we weren't up to the task. My dreams didn't come true this year. 1/4/87

A lot of guys will feel bad sitting around the TV watching the Giants, because we should be there. 1/6/87

**Two weeks later, brooding over how
winning a Super Bowl changes a team:**
The thing that changes, I think is not so much the people as it's maybe your incentive for getting (to the Super Bowl). The importance of it, maybe that's what I'm trying to say. It doesn't seem as important. Once you're in the Super Bowl, the game can never be what it's built up to be. The other day I read the great Duane Thomas quote, "If it's the ultimate game, why is there going to be another one next year?" That struck home. There's gonna be one every year and we're gonna be back in it. 1/5/87 Des Plaines Daily Herald

1987: A Season of Unpleasant Surprises

**Prior to the 1987 draft, Ditka felt that
the Bears had plenty of quarterbacks:**
We have quarterbacks we can go to the Super Bowl with. 4/26/87

I've heard stories we're going to draft a quarterback. I think that would be a silly draft. I'm really not in favor of drafting a quarterback. 4/29/87 Chicago Sun Times

**Jim Harbaugh, Michigan's quarterback, was
the Bears' No.1 selection. Ditka's reaction:**
We did a great job for our offense, we confused everybody and ourselves. 4/29/87 Des Plaines Daily Herald

A Different Season in '87

**Ditka felt the Bears were distracted by a number of events
during the 1986 season, particularly the acquisition of Flutie:**
We're going to play great football in 1987, and the fans are going to be tremendously proud of the players and what they accomplish on

the football field and we're going to keep all the other stuff out of the newspapers. 1/20/87

The comfort zone is over. There becomes a thing called the comfort zone with some players. They think they have been here, and so they always are going to be here. That's not true. We've made significant player changes. Look at the team pictures up on the wall, and see how many players we've changed. We can make the changes again that will enable us to win the Super Bowl. It's not a threat. It's a fact. I think we stood pat a little too much last year, but with good football players and good guys who worked their rear ends off. Now I wonder if we don't have guys with more talent at some positions, and maybe little younger guys, and we'll have to make those moves. There's no more comfort zone. 7/21/87

CAMP BEGINS

I want it to be like it was in '84 and '85, where we had to scratch and claw a little bit. We played reckless, with a chip on our shoulder. We challenged people. I want to go back to challenging people. No more Mr. Nice Guy. We had a couple of people play us like thugs the last couple of years. We're going to play any way they want to play. 6/2/87 Southtown Economist

We're the sleepers in the National Football Conference. We went to sleep for a year. We're back. 7/26/87 Chicago Sun Times

THE QUARTERBACK SITUATION

It's especially tough to have injuries at the quarterback position. Go in with a plan that says this guy is going to be here, and when he's not around you have to start switching around. We'll know right off the bat if Jim's well. If he is well and gets hurt, I still think the preparation going into the games will be better for the people who are behind him at quarterback and we'll be a better team. 7/22/87

OPENING AGAINST THE GIANTS

As if by fate, the first game of the 1987 season matched the 1986 Super Bowl champion New York Giants against the Bears, in Chicago. Ditka was asked how he felt about it:
It doesn't matter. You have to play somebody. Nobody can say we're limping into the season. We'll be diving right in. 4/12/87

I bet not one son-of-a-gun in Russia is watching. It's not a global conflict and it's not the ultimate game. 9/14/87

We had something to prove. All we proved is we won one game. 9/17/87

After the Bucs defeated the Bears 20-3:
That's a good football team. They make it awfully tough for us to get our job done. Our defense again was outstanding. 9/21/87

THE PLAYERS STRIKE

I don't know about anybody else, but I assume there is going to be no disruption in our football season. For me to sit here and say that there would be a disruption, I think I would be doing a disservice to myself and the fans and players. I can't do that. If there is a disruption, it's something I know nothing about and I really don't care about it. I just don't want to be involved in that aspect of it.
9/10/87 *Chicago Sun Times*

It happens in all walks of life. I was raised in a steel mill town. My dad went through one of the longest strikes in the steel industry. I don't know what it accomplished. Evidently, they thought it accomplished something. 9/20/87

When told the striking Bears would be conducting their own practices led by Mike Singletary, Ditka was skeptical:
You ought to find out where they're practicing and you ought to see

it there's 45 out there every day. I'll bet you there aren't. On any day. Are we talking about togetherness? Unity? Don't give me that crap. Because there's no discipline involved in it. We live in a world of discipline. *9/24/87 Chicago Sun Times*

THE STRIKE SEASON AND THE SPARE BEARS

The owners decision to field non-union teams created much controversy. Ditka was philosophical:
We're all part of the American dream. I'm just happy to be working, believe me. There's enough coaches out of work now. We don't need the ones working out of work. I don't feel like somebody's pulling the rug out from under me. For one day I felt that way, then I realized life goes on. I'm kind of happy.
9/25/87 Chicago Sun Times

When asked if he would be treating his non-union players differently from the real Bears:
The only thing I'll do different is I won't yell at anybody. I'll say "please" a lot more and fear that somebody will walk away and not come back. 9/22/87 *Chicago Sun Times*

This is a real work ethic group, a bunch of lunch bucket guys. No Gucci shoes in this outfit, gang. No Guccis.
10/13/87 Chicago Sun Times

The Strike Season Begins

SAINTS 19 — BEARS 17

I take every game in football seriously. Maybe their counterparts on strike don't think it means anything. But it means a lot to the young men who are out there playing. We instill that in them and we're proud of that. We're proud of being the Chicago Bears. We're proud of what the game stands for and what it will always stand for. We're not about to go around bitching and griping about things that don't make any difference. These kids don't gripe about anything. We hauled them out at 5 o'clock in the morning Sunday and they were there and they went into the locker room and went to sleep. They got up, went upstairs and ate a pregame meal. All unusual circumstances. And they loved it. Then they went out on the field and played like hell. Our defense looked the same to me. If you take the names off the jerseys and change the numbers around, you'd never recognize the difference. 10/6/87

THE STRIKING BEARS

There can be strength in unity, but there can also be stupidity. How much do you think [Bear] players get along together? You think they get phone calls every night from their teammates saying, "Why don't you come over and play checkers?" Once they leave here, how many of them talk with each other? We have guys who don't talk to anybody. So what difference does it make? I don't see these guys socializing much. A few guys get a beer together, but other than that, they all scatter. 10/6/87

When told his prediction that some of the Bears would fail to show for the impromptu practices was correct:
We have some of the laziest guys who are non-motivated in the world. They get a lot of credit, you know, and that in itself should show a lot of players who do show up—they don't really care about them. There's no togetherness. It's all for themselves. The egos rule. We have a tremendous amount of egomaniacs. And the only way you control egomaniacs is with discipline. The better word in the dictionary calls it prima donna. She don't dance on this field. She don't sing in this theater. But she's around, if you let her be. My frame of mind right now is not good. I wonder if the coaches in the NFL should tell them [the players] to stick it. Of course, the players don't need coaches. We all know that. They can play without us. You know how well they played here for years. They're super without coaching; they can do whatever they want. 9/29/87

I hope my players know what I think of them. I respect them tremendously. They're fighting for a cause they think is right. I don't know who is right or wrong anymore. 10/12/87 *Chicago Sun Times*

THE STRIKE ENDS: THE VOTE AND THE VETO

Ditka let his regular players decide whether the non-union Bears could become regular Bears. It was reported that the vote was 44-1 against the non-union Bears. Ditka rejected the decision:
I let them vote because I thought they'd be realistic about it. If someone could help our team, I thought they'd let them. But they saw fit not to do that. The only thing I worry about is winning games. I'm not in a popularity contest. A lot of those guys made a lot of decisions the past four weeks. I'm the boss now. I make the decisions and live with them. 10/21/87

BITTER BEARS

Dennis McKinnon:
The family got vetoed. It doesn't make any difference what we say. We found out we had no power. The family structure holds no water. We're 45 guys who are gonna go out and win. We're gonna do our best to win the Super Bowl. And this time it will be a player who will be carrying the Super Bowl and not management.
10/22/87 Chicago Sun Times

Jim McMahon:
At the time Mike[Ditka] said we'd vote. Michael McCaskey turned around like he was surprised. It probably wasn't the smartest thing to do. At the time it was, "If you guys don't want them (non-union players) we won't keep 'em. It's as simple as that." Well, I guess it's not. 10/22/87 *Chicago Sun Times*

THE REAL SEASON BEGINS: THE GREAT GUMBALL CAPER

**San Francisco police officer George
Pohley filed this report about the incident:**
*As I was escorting Coach Ditka from the playing field, he stopped
and looked at the people sitting in the pullout seats. He then took a
piece of gum from his mouth and threw it at the victim, reported
Ornelas, striking her in the back of the head. Coach Ditka then flipped
the bird with his left hand and exited the field.*
12/16/87 Chicago Sun Times

Ditka responded:
Any time anybody throws something at me, I'm going to throw
something back. 12/16/87 *Chicago Sun Times*

Diana Ditka on the incident:
*She [the woman] was lucky Mike didn't have a bat in his hand. He'd
have thrown it. 12/16/87* Chicago Sun Times

**Mark Rodenhauser, Bears center commenting
on the unbelievable nature of the whole incident,
especially booking the gum as evidence:**
That's ridiculous. What are they gonna charge: Assault with a deadly
gumball? 12/16/87

**During breakfast in the hotel restaurant the morning after
the game, Ken Valdiserri, Bears publicist, approached Mike
and Diana Ditka. Diana Ditka explains their conversation:**
*Kenny told Mike there was a group of reporters wanting to speak to
him about the gum thing. Mike said, "What for?" Kenny then told
him the lady was planning to press charges. That's when Mike blew
up, and why not? I see she's changed her mind; she's not going to
carry this dumb thing any further. All she wants is some sort of
apology, I guess. Well, what about Mike and our players? Don't
they get an apology for the way they were treated? They were like
sitting ducks out there Monday night. The fans are right on top of*

you in that park, and they throw everything. Does this lady admit she threw a cup of ice at Mike as he was leaving the field after the game? Of course not. But she's gotten her name in the papers and her face on TV, so that's all she cares about. Those fans are awful out there. There were cops on horseback on the field after the game, and still the fans came out of the stands. Imagine what would have happened if the 49ers had lost. 12/17/87

In the week after the 49ers game, the 49ers announced that action would be taken against individuals that harass visiting teams. Also, Bill Walsh telephoned Mike Ditka to apologize for the behavior of the fans:
Mike was a gentleman about it. Mike minimized it to me; I maximized it to him. 12/21/87

1987 Playoffs

REDSKINS 21, BEARS 17

The Redskins eliminated the Bears from the play-offs. Turnovers and the inability to capitalize on opportunities led to the Bears defeat, their third defeat in the last four games. At the end of the game Walter Payton, playing for the last time, sat dejectedly after all the players had left. Ditka:
I want to congratulate the Redskins and wish both teams (Minnesota also) the best of luck. They've worked hard and they both deserve it; they earned it. It's a credit to the Minnesota football team and to the Washington football team. I think very simply, in a nutshell—I won't belabor the point because I don't want to be up here very long—we ain't good enough right now, gang, it's that simple. We had a number of opportunities, but when we have to stop people, we aren't capable of stopping people. And when we have to score or block people, we don't do a good enough job. Of course the inconsistencies and turnovers hurt us again, and we had some key opportunities to make some big plays and we didn't make 'em. We just are not good enough right now with the people we have or the way we're playing. So something's got to be changed. We'll all evaluate ourselves, coaches

and players, and I think that's where you go. It's not a dismal year; I mean it was a good year if you consider a lot of things that happened. There were a lot of good things. But when it goes two years in a row that you end up in this same position [losing the conference semifinal], it's not very much fun. I don't want to be in this position again. So it's about that simple. There's not much else to say. Our guys played hard. It wasn't a matter of wanting to; it wasn't a matter of being ready; it wasn't a matter of being stale. It was a matter of not being able to make the plays when you have to. They made a play on special teams and we didn't--it's that simple. It was a close game and I thought it would be. 1/11/88 Chicago Sun-Times

Ditka's view of the loss:
When it happens to you two years in a row it's not any fun. I don't want to be in this position again. If we can't do it with the people we have or the way we're playing, something has to be done. 1/11/88

CHANGES FOR THE 1988 SEASON

I'm tired of the lack of discipline, tired of people who think they have better answers and solutions because all of a sudden we win a few games. There are people who consider this drudgery, no fun to be around. That wasn't the case two years ago. It was fun to be here. My God, if you consider it drudgery, then don't do it. Do something else and see if we can make that kind of money doing something else in society. We can't. 1/12/88 Chicago Sun-Times

I've been in this game 27 years as a pro, and I know what it takes to win. The difference now is we have 50 experts instead of a couple. 1/12/88 *Southtown Economist*

We have to get back to the offseason conditioning program that we had here a couple of years ago when people thought it was important to work out. All of a sudden we're a bunch of individuals that all have their own gyms in their own house. They all work out at home--maybe they do, maybe they don't. 1/12/88 Chicago Sun-Times

THE 1988 SEASON

INJURIES AND A HEART ATTACK

Offense 1988

You've got to realize this is no longer a team that's going to be dominated by Walter Payton. I don't know that we're going to run that kind of offense anymore. We're going to try to run an offense that can utilize whatever people we have so [defenses] won't know when we're going to pass, when we're going to run. 4/25/88 Chicago Sun-Times

TRAINING CAMP

I've been a nice guy and I will continue to be a nice guy, but you've got to push some guys... The sun got me a little hot today, too. We've just got to get better, and that's my job. Right now we're not the best we can be. 8/17/88

It's easy to sit back and say, "When the time comes, we'll turn it on." It doesn't work that way. It doesn't work that way in life or football.

You just can't turn it on when you need it. You've got to build up to the point where it comes naturally. 8/18/88

After losing to Dallas 17-9 in the preseason:
Everybody is going to have their alibis and it becomes humorous to me because I've been around guys who alibi before in life and they say: Oh well, it's exhibition. It doesn't count. We're a little tired. We're coming out of camp...You'll hear every alibi in the world. We just played lousy. I mean it's embarrassing. I apologize. We won't play that bad again. 8/23/88

I said earlier this year when we went to training camp that this would be a transition year for the Bears. We'll find out if it's a good transition year or a bad one. But we're going to try to make it with the people we have. 8/30/88

KEY GAMES

After opening the season defeating the Miami Dolphins 34-7:
I don't put much stock in the first game... Our guys played as hard as they could. They made some good things happen. I was very proud of the effort all the way through. We will try to improve, and we'll try to meet the expectations of the experts [the media] in America. 9/5/88

VIKINGS 31 — BEARS 7

Football kind of mirrors life. We're down, but I don't think we'll stay down. We'll fight back. Whether we can be all that we want to be this year, I don't know. You (media) guys have a right to crow now. 9/19/88

BEARS 10 — 49ERS 9

I don't know how good we are; I don't care how good we are. If we continue to play with the attitude we had tonight, we'll make it interesting for everybody. 10/25/88

PATRIOTS 30 — BEARS 7

That was the worst football game that a Bears team has played since I've been here. We were absolutely annihilated. 12/30/88

Heart Attack

On November 2, 1988 Mike Ditka suffered a mild heart attack. Coach Ditka's family, friends, and players expressed concern that the strains of coaching might precipitate another more serious heart attack. Two weeks later he was back on the sidelines coaching against the Tampa Bay Buccaneers.

**Mike Ditka's wife, Diana Ditka, was asked what
she would tell her husband to do after his attack:**
I don't tell Mike Ditka anything. He gives me two choices: slim and none. 11/16/88

**Diana Ditka explained that Mike felt
"embarrassed" about his heart attack:**
I think he's saying to himself: "Did this really happen to me? I better take better care of myself." I really believe that he knows what he has to do now. It scared him, and it embarrassed him, too. He thought he was so healthy, and he thought that he did all the right things. And then to have that happen to him...he couldn't believe it was happening. 11/16/88

Excerpt from a fan in Andover, Massachusetts:
I'm going to start this off with the way I feel. I don't like you. I don't like the Bears. As a matter of fact, I detest you. But I want you to get better because you're good for football. 11/20/88

**Bear linebacker Mike Singletary's analysis of
Mike Ditka coaching for the first time after his heart attack:**
He's calm and a little more relaxed. There can be so many blessings in life and maybe this is one of them. Not that you wish a heart attack on anybody. Mike is a very wise man. He's effective in different situations and in different ways. 11/25/88

**Former Bear general manager and long
time Ditka friend, Jerry Vainisi:**

*I think the heart attack made him pause. He's changed his lifestyle
quite a bit. ...I know he has changed his eating habits and his lifestyle,
somewhat. And those changes, I'm sure are for the better. He knows
what he's got to do. 9/20/89*

REFLECTIONS ON THE HEART ATTACK

**When reminded by the media of statements he made about
changing his personality after his heart attack Ditka responded:**
I lie a lot. 10/29/89

*Do I sit back and dwell on it? No. But I think about it every time I
get a funny feeling. Any time I get any kind of feeling, I think, "I
wonder if it has anything do with that?" Everytime I got feelings
before, I never thought it meant anything. 10/29/89*

Former Bear teammate Ed O'Bradovich:
Nothing has changed since 1962. You want to play golf with him?
You don't relax; it's torture. He thrives on this stuff. I think all the
frustration and anger are part of his enjoyment. If he sat in Florida,
read books and walked along the beach, then he might die. 10/29/89

Diana Ditka:
*I was ready to kill him last summer and say he died of natural causes.
I called Dr. Alexander and asked, "What can I give him to calm him
down?" He said, "An elephant gun." But I'm starting to see he's
been calmer. He's not drinking, and he has a nice sense of humor.
But you can't change your personality. You can change eating habits
and work habits, but you can't change your personality. 10/29/89*

OVERCOMING A LACK OF TALENT

1989 To 1992
A New Ditka in 1989?

I am much more personable a guy. I'm laid-backed and relaxed. I don't let anything get me excited anymore. The outward appearance may change a few things, but if you ever change your intensity about what's important in life, get out of it, do something else. I can't do that. 8/14/89

REGULAR SEASON

After winning the first four regular season games, Ditka reflected on his team:
We don't ever want to change our focus; we don't ever change our goal. I'm not saying that we will reach every goal that we set, but we don't ever change that. I'm not surprised, but I think there would be a lot of people who are surprised that we could be 4-0 after these

*four games, playing Cincinnati, Minnesota, and Philadelphia. But it
happened. We must be awfully lucky. 10/3/89*

**After losing the first game of the season
to the Tampa Bay Buccaneers 42-35:**
We probably were outcoached. I don't think we handled the situations
we had very well with our defense and offense. But I give [Tampa
Bay] all the credit. I don't take anything away from them. Evidently,
we're very stereotyped about a lot of things we're doing because
they seemed to know what we were doing. The only thing I can say
about our guys is they hung in there and they tried. We were outplayed
and outcoached. 10/9/89

**The following week the Bears lost again to the
Houston Oilers 33-28, giving up two touchdowns
in the final five minutes of the game:**
*Now I don't know if we're capable of winning another football game.
I don't think we are at this point. This football team is in disarray
and we are not very good. We looked at some of our key guys for
leadership and I'm not sure I see it. Maybe we aren't as tough as I
thought we were. I always thought we were pretty tough, but I don't
know. 10/16/89*

Bear linebacker Mike Singletary's reaction to Ditka's outburst:
That's the only thing that scares me when he acts like that. But you
can't take the frustration out of a guy. You can't take that attitude
away from him. 10/23/89

*Other teams are laughing, giggling, having fun. To the victor goes
the spoils. If you can't win, you can't laugh. Lots of teams will laugh
[at the Bears] now. That's okay. Let them take their shots now. If
we had Dan Hampton and Richard Dent healthy, we could play
defense with anyone. But we haven't had them. We're not a dominant
team, but that doesn't mean we can't win football games. 10/25/89*

Because these are my players, these are the players I have developed,
that I want here, that I drafted here. So it is my fault. I can't blame

anyone else. I take full blame for it. When you take enough blame and get enough blame over a period of time...like Ricochet Rabbit, you're gone. 10/25/89

Everybody wants to give you credit for what you accomplish in life. To me you measure people by what they overcome in life, how they react to situations that aren't good. 10/25/89

**When told that Diana Ditka said that
he seemed more intense this season than ever:**
In some things, she is probably right. I know why it is in football. I get disturbed about people not appreciating it and not busting their butt in football for what they get out of it. A lot do, but those that don't and want to gripe about what they don't have instead of appreciating what they do have, bothers me. 10/29/89

It seems like everybody wants to treat football as a business. The business of life is to produce or get on about your life. We have to do more producing in certain areas. And the individuals who have to do it know that. There are no hard feelings by anybody, no matter what is said by me or anybody else. This is our job, this is what we're paid to do. Let's go out and do it to the best of our ability. 10/31/89

THE SEASON'S FRUSTRATIONS: HINTS AT LEAVING?

Sometimes in life, you know, honesty is appreciated, sometimes it's not. I've always tried to be honest from the day I got the job until now. There was a while when people appreciated...and now that we've had some success, people don't appreciate honesty anymore. You're supposed to tell them what they want to hear. Well it won't be that way and I don't think they will have to worry about it very long. They can get somebody else and continue about their own ways. And the Bears will continue to win because the blocks are in place. 11/8/89

**When asked by the media if he was
seriously considering leaving coaching:**

*I said it, and what I said, I mean. I said maybe it's time for a change.
I said a lot of things. I'm very frustrated right now. I'm bothered. I
hate to lose. I hate the way we look. I hate the way it feels. I don't
like it. I'd like to change it, not by running away from it. But if I
thought someone else could handle it better than I can, I'd step aside.
My main concern is not me, it's the Bears. A lot of other people seem
to think it's me, but it's not it's the Bears. 11/28/89*

That would be a great honor to be able to finish out my contract
[until 1990]. I've said it a thousand times that when the fire is not
burning anymore; it's not burning. Right now, it's burning. Matter
of fact, it was burning too much. 11/30/89

Bears President Michael McCaskey:

*There is no doubt in my mind that Mike Ditka is the right guy to be
coaching the Chicago Bears. I've said that over and over again.
There is no one who matches the character of the team quite so much
as Mike. 12/24/89*

MORE FRUSTRATIONS

If I were to put my finger on one thing, we don't have any team
speed on defense. Anybody want to argue that? 12/19/89

Bears President Michael McCaskey:

*Personally, my own style is to keep a more positive approach to things.
When the going gets tough, you want to encourage people. Help
them find the strength to battle back. He (Ditka) has been very
successful over the years working both the pat-on-the-back and
motivating by fear. I think this time around he hit the fear side too
hard, which was not so important when we were winning and we had
veteran players. But now we have a lot of younger players and they
didn't know quite how to react. 12/15/89*

Diana Ditka:
Mike has always been fired up, as long as I've known him. He has yelled at players and at coaches. But when you lose, I guess people want to criticize something or put the blame on something. He is not going to change. When he doesn't yell on the sidelines, they say he can't motivate. You lose either way, unless you're winning. You can't lose injured players and expect a young team to win. I think he really felt like they were going to win. 12/25/89

Bears special teams coach, Steve Kazor on Ditka's temper:
When we were winning all those years, nobody ever noticed it. Now when you lose, everybody tries to nit-pick at the little things as to why we lost. He used to get excited about players on the field. You have pictures of him grabbing guys' face masks, getting in my ear a couple of times. If I had a dollar for every time he cussed me out I wouldn't be here; it would have been like winning the Lotto. 9/9/90

What have I learned this year? There it is, written on that plaque, "Failure is not fatal; success is not permanent." When you succeed, you find out an awful lot of people want to see you fail. 12/22/89

49ers 26 — BEARS 0
I guess when you hit bottom—and we hit it today—I guess you just gotta bounce. I believe we'll bounce... Somewhere along the line we lost our confidence and believing in what we could do. I didn't believe we were that bad a football team, but I think a lot of people want to believe that. I guess you've got to believe it after today... We've had a lot of great seasons and this happens to be one we have to forget about. We can toast the past and we can taste the future. We just have to forget about this year. 12/25/89

A New Year — 1990

We are trying to win; that is all we are trying to accomplish. We are trying to win and get some continuity and see how we are playing on offense and defense. See if we can correct a couple of problems we had last year, be a little more effective in the control passing game. Run the ball some. Try not to give as many big plays. Those would be the things that I would look at. 8/4/90

Bears offensive coordinator Greg Landry:
I just look at last year as a little blip, something that was unfortunate. When I look back at Mike Ditka in the years I have been here, he is an excellent man to work for. 8/8/90

I think that in some ways things will be a little different this year. I don't want to get into exactly how they will be different. But my approach is only to put the best team on the field that I can to make the fans and the players proud of what we're doing. If you do it and it works, people are going to say, 'Gosh, he's a genius.' If it doesn't work, they will say, 'He's a bum.' We live in a society that has a tendency to build people up and tear them down. 8/19/90

I'm an optimist, and I have a better attitude. We can go nose-to-nose with anybody and play awfully well if we don't end up with a bunch of injuries. I don't think there is going to be a dominant team, and we can fit in with the rest of them. 9/7/90

THE REGULAR SEASON

BEARS 31 — PACKERS 13

They are playing hard, they're trying. I wouldn't sell the house yet, but we're trying to keep it in line. 9/17/90

I don't think there are many people right even right now who really respect this team. That's the way I like it. That's the way I want it. The players just want to keep going out and proving it. That's what is important in life---not what people think of you, but what you think of yourself. If you think enough of yourself, you'll make the guy you're playing against think you're good, too. 10/16/90

VIKINGS 41 — BEARS 13

I don't feel as bad as probably a lot of people think I should. Once the truck hit me, I didn't bother getting up. I just lay there and watched. 11/26/90

Getting beat happens to anybody. Staying beat, you can do something about that. We have control over what we do from here on out. 11/26/90

BEARS 23 — LIONS 17

A year ago we couldn't have won this game... It is the attitude of this football team; it is the attitude of those men. They are playing hard and they believe in what the heck they are doing, that's all. Win or lose, you can't fault the effort. 12/3/90

I think we've been too nice lately. We need to play meaner, with a chip on our shoulder. 12/21/90

Even with a 11-5 record football experts were skeptical on the Bears chances for success in the playoffs:
People are writing us off. They say, "You can't win" and "You have no quarterback." We'll see what we have. We have to do the best we can. We didn't ask to get in this situation, but that's part of football... You don't know what is going to happen. But we have to play with the hand we're dealt and we are just going to do the best we can with it. 12/23/90

PLAYOFFS

You always position yourself in life for this. Period. The season means nothing. They don't give no trophies for the season. No rings. No awards. No money. The season puts you in a position to say that you can accomplish something special. We got in that position and New Orleans got in that position. That is all the season is about. You must make the playoffs. Once you make the playoffs, it becomes a second season and then anybody can do anything. 1/3/91

A NEW AWARENESS

But this is the closest team I have seen, and the closest group off the field. They do more things together, like golfing and bowling. They fit in with each other. It seems they are having more fun that we have had the last couple of years. I don't know if we are having more fun that we had in '85. That was a lot of fun. We won the Super Bowl. In the past we had friction, no question about it. We went through strikes, and there were a lot of things said in those meetings that probably offended people. There are no real controversies around here anymore. I attribute that to the team concept. I can't say this is etched in stone, but as long as we do the things we are doing, we have a chance to stay that way. 10/19/90

Bear lineman, Richard Dent:
I have been talking to Mike about being more in contact with the players. Some coaches don't like getting too close because you have players going on and off the team. But the more a player feels in tune with you, the more they are going to produce for you. That's something I mentioned to him. It can only make a team stronger. We play cards and stuff on the plane, just little things. The little things always mean a lot. 10/19/90

I've always been sensitive to [player concerns]. But sometimes you have to think about it. When you do things a certain way a long time and have success, it is very hard to back off. But as long as I see the effort in practice, I don't see a lot of reason to do a lot of extra stuff. We're all on the same bus going to the same place. If we all want to get there, we have to pull together. But sometimes the coach does have a little better perception of what the right things are. 10/19/90

**Bear cornerback, Vestee Jackson on the difference
between the Mike Ditka of 1989 and the Ditka of 1990:**
[Ditka] realized at the time that communication had totally broken down amongst the team. Not only with myself, but with several other guys. I think he has learned from that, as well as everyone else on

the team. The [sign] he has on his desk is 'Communication.' His door is always open for anyone who wants to speak. If they want to go in and tell Ditka off, or what have you, he is open to hear that. 10/31/90

REFLECTIONS ON THE SEASON

I'm not a Chuck Noll or Don Shula or a Joe Gibbs. I don't want to coach forever. But I also decided last off-season that I want to coach at least a couple more years and I don't want to leave on a 6-10 note. Could I have handled another 6-10 year this year? Oh, I could have handled it, but that doesn't mean I would have been back. I'm 51, and I've always wanted to draw the line at 55. Who's to say at 55, I won't be enjoying it more than ever? Or at 53, that I wake up one morning and decide, that's it, I don't want to go to the office anymore. It's that I haven't reached that point yet. Why not take a shot at doing what I want to do where I want to do it? Chicago, I'm the perfect guy for the job? They could find someone else to replace me, but the question is, could I go anyplace else except the Bears? I can't speak for Bill Walsh, but I bet one week after he retired from the 49ers, he regretted it. I don't want to be like that, I want to be sure. 1/5/91

1991 — The Regular Season

After beating the Bucs 21-20 to go 2-0:
I'm happy with the win but... I understand basics, and I understand what it takes. Right now, we're not there. We're not on page 1 yet. I mean, we're way back in the comics section at this point. 9/9/91

Going for his 100th career win against the Jets:
You keep it in the back of your mind. But records that are accomplished like that are not individual records anyway. They are a direct result of team play. Right now we are playing well as a team and that is the only thing I have tried to get across. 9/23/91

The Bears beat the Jets 19-13 in overtime:
We may be the luckiest team in the world. It might be devine intervention. 9/24/91

REDSKINS 20 — BEARS 7:

We lost to a pretty good football team. I guess I could be a philosopher and tell you things and this and that. But we lost to a pretty good football team. They deserved to beat us; they are better than we are. If we would have beat them, it would have been a tremendous upset. We are not as good as they are, and that is fact. 10/7/91

BEARS 10 — PACKERS 0

I'm glad to have a win. I don't care what it looks like. I ain't apologizing and I'm not giving it back. It's fun; it's great. Our offense isn't scoring, so we're going to have to shut out a lot of people. 10/18/91

BEARS 20 — SAINTS 17

A lot of people are going to criticize this kind of football game. This was good football. Man, this is what football is all about—people getting the snot knocked out of them. 10/28/91

When asked how close he was to retiring:
If I feel I don't have the type of players I want, the type of discipline I want, then, yes, I will walk away from it. 12/6/91

Is it all right to be an emotional player and not an emotional coach? I'm going to have an emotional performance myself. I haven't had one this year yet. 12/6/91

PROBLEMS IN DECEMBER:

I would rather talk about the sunshine rather than the rain coming. But it is evident over the years that our problem in December has been basically at the quarterback position. A lot of teams go through that, too. And they still win. Maybe it's lousy coaching. 12/8/91

PLAYOFFS
— — — —

I would say right now that Dallas rates right at the top of the teams that are in the playoffs. We're probably at the bottom right now. We're probably going in with the biggest strikes against us. But I will say this: Beware. We didn't get to be 11-5 by using mirrors. We are a good football team. We were not a good football team Monday night [in the loss to the 49ers]. And I believe this team will prove it is a good football team before the playoffs are over. 12/27/91

DALLAS 17 — BEARS 13
Our guys played hard and they tried. There was no lack of effort. [Dallas] won, that's all. If you want to fault somebody, I guess you have to fault me. Don't fault those guys. They fought like heck. If you want to be analytical about it, maybe we are a step away. We'll find out how to make that step up. But maybe that's where we are. Maybe we don't belong up there with these other [playoff] people. 12/30/91

CHANGES IN 1992:
— — — — — — — — —

I'm meeting with players, individually. I'm going to explain to players what I want to do, what I want to incorporate in the off-season, what I expect from them personally. 12/31/91

When asked if his laid-back style in 1991
had a negative effect on the team:
There's no question about it. I felt that I would try to look at the important things and try to overlook some of the unimportant things. But what is unimportant? If it has to do with discipline, everything is important...I did mellow too far. I think that I became so worried about the Mike Ditka image of getting excited and getting angry at times that I became this guy who didn't get excited and didn't get angry at the right times. I think excitement and anger are good if justifiable. 12/31/91

The 1992 Season

We're a better football team right now than we were in our second preseason game in 1985. That's all I can tell you. If we can get better than that, that would be nice. That would be great. We're playing better as a team. Not that we have better individuals. Those individuals in '85 were pretty good. But they weren't playing as a team in the second preseason game like we are now. And we will get better. 8/18/92

Analyzing the 1991 season:
To accomplish things that we did this year with the people we had playing, and we had to play them, and the number of injuries we had, I think we did a very good job. Did we do the best job? No, we could have done a little better job. But we did a pretty good job, and I think that is a credit to the players. Period. 1/5/92

My enthusiasm is the best it's been in 10 years because I think we're a much better football team than we ended up last year. 9/4/92

REGULAR SEASON

SAINTS 28 — BEARS 6:
It's going to be a long season. 9/14/92

On the Bears players poor execution in the loss to the Saints:
What am I going to do? I mean, I could go back and grab the guy, choke him, scourge him at the cross, eulogize him and bury him. I'm not going to do that. That doesn't do any good. This is my team. This is our team. This is who I have to play with. Now, if it's not good enough, that's my fault. Because I kept them here. 9/15/92

After two losses in the first three games:
We're trying to have fun. Sometimes it's hard to smile when you have tears in your eyes. But this football team is not down. This is not a demoralized team. It is not a team that doesn't believe in itself. 9/25/92

BEARS 41 — FALCONS 31

I'm a realist; not a phony. I understand where the problems are and we're trying to find solutions to the problems. We've got to play better if we expect to win a lot of football games. 9/28/92

VIKINGS 21 — BEARS 20

We haven't changed much, I guess. We haven't figured out how to play 60 minutes of football. That's kind of bothersome. 10/5/95

On Bear quarterback Jim Harbaugh's audible leading to a Viking interception late in the 4th quarter:

I will say this honestly—if the situation arises again, there will be changes made and they will be permanent. I'm not going to put 47 guys' careers in the hands of somebody who thinks he knows more than I know. That's the way I feel. 10/5/92

Jim Harbaugh's response:

It's Mike's team; he can do whatever he wants to. 10/5/92

VIKINGS 38 — BEARS 10

We got thoroughly whipped. And we have to give them all the credit in the world. They did a great job, and we kind of never got into the flow of what we wanted to do. I told the football team that we're better than we played. But we've got to prove that. We have to go back and start digging out of the ditch again. There's a long time left in the season. There's no use for anybody on our team or in our organization being down. 11/3/92

BENGALS 31 — BEARS 28

If you can't win a football game like that [blowing a 14-point lead in the 4th quarter], then you don't have a right to win. We have a lot of people who try hard and we have some who don't look like they understand what it's all about. No pointing fingers. It's just a team game. 11/9/92

Ex-Bear Jay Hilgenberg, starting center for the Browns:
Here in Cleveland, all you hear about is stuff about Coach Ditka and whether he should coach anymore. I think that is a little crazy to hear. Because Coach Ditka is a great football coach. The one thing to make a good football player and a good team is pride. And that is one thing Mike Ditka has an awful lot of. He instills that in his players. To get a new coach in Chicago, I think would be crazy right now. 11/10/92

BUCCANEERS 20 — BEARS 17
Bears tackle Stan Thomas:
Coach Ditka was very quiet at halftime. He has tried everything. He has tried getting everybody pumped up at halftime. That is the usual routine. But today he was very strange. Kind of quiet. He told us we know what we have got to do when we walked out. 11/16/92

Bear quarterback Jim Harbaugh:
Everybody is trying to do their job as well as they can. The same with Coach Ditka. I think it is frustrating for him right now because he can't walk across those lines and play football. The game plans are there. The game plans are good. We are lacking in execution at times. Coach Ditka is the guy who gets blamed a lot and has people throwing stuff on him, screaming obscenities at him. And he is probably the last person to blame at this point. 11/18/92

Bear tight end, Keith Jennings:
If coach Ditka could go out and play right now to help us win, I bet he would suit up. He is that type of man. He's tough. I've got to give him credit. And I have only been here two years. I have never in my life had a coach like that. He's real tough. He has made me tougher. He has made me look at football totally different. 11/19/92

LIONS 16 — BEARS 3
The difference is not emotion so much, it's execution. We didn't execute. You can't blame it on emotion. 12/21/92

**When asked by the media about the teams
inability to get emotional for the Lions game:**
That's bull, that's corn, that's nothing. It's playing, it's covering, it's hitting, it's tackling, it's running, it's executing on offense. And we didn't do those things. It's not the emotion, it's the execution. 12/21/92

COWBOYS 27 — BEARS 14

Regardless of what happens, it has been a helluva run. I told someone earlier, I'm not sure where the line is to apologize. But wherever it is, I won't be in it. It has been a helluva run. I've enjoyed it... So we will see what happens. I'm an optimist. I believe in the best. I know one thing: I'm a Bear. Whether people like it or not, I'm a Bear. 12/28/92

REFLECTIONS ON THE 1992 SEASON

**When a reporter mentioned that 1992 was the first season
since 1975 that a Bear wasn't selected for the Pro Bowl:**
I don't really worry too much about that. I didn't worry about it when we won the Super Bowl, either. It never entered my mind, because you do things as a team. It's never the coach, it's never the individual player. It's the whole concept of what you're doing. 12/27/92

Production is the name of the game. Results. If we can put the team back on course and get everybody on the same page and maybe get a little help in certain areas, it can be done... I believe anything can be done if you put your mind to it. What your mind can conceive and your heart can believe, you can achieve. That's an old saying, but I believe it. 12/27/92

**Jerry Fontenot, a Bear in 1992 and a Saint in 1997,
responded to a New Orleans reporter's question
about the failure of the 1992 Bears:**
I think there was a fall-off in talent. From my observation, Mike

seemed frustrated with some of the picks in the draft, and he didn't have as much control of that as he probably should have had. That made for a difficult situation. You can do so much with the talent we had. In order to compete and win at the championship level, you have to measure yourself against the top teams in the league. At that point, talent-wise, I don't think we could stand up to a lot of the better teams. 8/14/97 *New Orleans Times-Picayune*

Bear President Mike McCaskey:
We have to find some new ways to do some things very differently from the way we've done them in the past. 1/6/93

Bear President Mike McCaskey Mike Ditka has meant a great deal to this ballclub and we are appreciative. If I had my druthers, I wish we could have ended his career with the Bears in a blaze of glory. 1/6/93

When asked how close he came to extending Mike Ditka's contract McCaskey replied:
I would say it was a tough decision. Everybody knows what strong contributions Mike Ditka has made to the Chicago Bears. He helped restore pride to the Chicago Bears uniform. He took a lot of key ingredients that Jim Finks and others put into place, added to it and helped us get to the Super Bowl. So it's very tough to say to a coach who's done that for you: Things haven't been going to well lately, and it's to a point where we needed to make a change. 1/7/93

McCaskey when asked about Ditka's complaint about having more authority:
It didn't play much of a role, but it showed an improper anaylsis. He had a lot of authority in the areas he was talking about. He had chosen and hired all the coaches on his staff. 1/7/93

MIKE DITKA'S FAREWELL SPEECH

I will try to do this with class, if I can. The Scriptures tell you that all things shall pass. This, too, shall pass. Regrets...just a few. They are too few to remember... I have a lot of people to thank. I have a lot of coaches that I have worked for over the years, as a player, as an assistant coach. I thank Coach [George Halas]. I guess you have got to thank the players the most because they make it happen. I was blessed. I came here and inherited a hell of a football team... Disagreements or no disagreements, they have been very vital to my life. I have had my run-ins with you [media] guys and I have had a lot of support from you. I appreciate it and I thank you. I thank the fans of this city. You know, the Bears will come back. Mike Ditka will survive. I will land on my feet. There is no problem about that. I don't worry about that. I worry about how this organization is perceived. I believe we will go forward and try to do the things that are necessary to get through the '90s the way it should. I would hope that. It is hard to erase 17 years. Nothing much else to say. But thank you, I appreciate it. But this, too, shall pass. 1/6/93

THE REACTION

Chicago Mayor Richard Daley:
Mike Ditka has been a great symbol for this city. He has the toughness that this city needs in this day and age, and he's always had it... I wouldn't have fired him. 1/6/93

Defensive backfield coach, Zaven Yaralian:
It's a sad day for football, believe me. 1/6/93

Offensive line coach, Dick Stanfel:
They judged Mike on maybe two years and not the other nine. He had nine great years here. It's very unfair to him. It's an empty feeling, a really empty feeling. I think he's a great coach, a great motivator. When you see a man's life really end in this area, it just kind of hurts, that's all. 1/6/93

Former Bear Dan Hampton:
Anybody that cared about the Bears will be wearing black armbands around. It will be hard to think about the Bears without thinking of Mike Ditka. 1/6/93

Bear defensive lineman Steve McMichael:
[Ditka] was made a scapegoat for a bunch of guys who were not doing the job on the field. If they'd done it right, they'd have fired all the players instead of the coach. It's the players fault; we bear it on our shoulders. 1/12/93

Jim McMahon:
Most of the time we argued but we both wanted to win. I would have liked to have played with him. He's the kind of guy you'd want on your team. He would've had a different opinion of me if he'd been in the huddle with me. He gave everything to the game, and that's the same way he coached. I respect him as a man, no doubt about it. You always knew where you stood with the guy. 1/15/93

John Evasovich, a Ditka boyhood friend:
Mike Ditka to me is integrity, honesty, caring—someone who is confident in himself. He is unpretentious, and Mike knows Mike better than anybody. Ditka was Chicago. When you said Chicago, those of us outside the city didn't think of Mayor Daley or anything else. We thought of either Michael Jordan or Mike Ditka. 1/15/93

Ken Geiger, Bears scout:
He's a competitive person who won't settle for anything but the best. He's a great human being, but other people never got to see the other

side of him. He's one of the most generous people I've ever met. When a close mutual friend got out of the hospital one time, Mike took him into his home for six weeks. 1/15/93

Mike Tomczak:
I respect Mike Ditka a lot more I do than Mike McCaskey. 1/15/93

Mary Albright, Mike Ditka's secretary:
The bear that he was, there was still this generosity because he cared so much. The humanitarian side of his personality, the unselfishness and his sensitivity overshadowed the grizzly. He always had time for others. His office door was open to all people no matter what their position or status in life, especially the disadvantaged and handicapped. 1/15/93

Jerry Fontenot was asked by a New Orleans reporter in 1997 how he felt about the treatment of Ditka, in 1992, by the Chicago media and Bear owner Mike McCaskey:
It was a reality check for me, because he had been so successful in Chicago. The way he was released really caught us all by surprise. We didn't expect Mike to be released...When he left, there was a big level of disappointment... I still have a lot of respect for him for doing that. If that happened to him, it certainly could happen to any of us, no matter how long you had been with the team. At any given point, you're out there fighting for your job.
8/14/97 *New Orleans Times-Picayune*

DITKA'S FINAL BEAR THOUGHTS

I really believed I can orchestrate the turnaround. I tried to talk him [McCaskey] into that fact, but he made up his mind, and I'm not real good at begging. 1/7/93

I'll take another run at it somewhere. To say I'm depressed, I'd be a liar. We won the Super Bowl. The feeling there was elation and relief. Maybe some of this is relief, I don't know. 1/6/93

*I wish it would have been handled differently. I think I was entitled
to have it handled differently, me and my coaches. I don't really
believe this came about because of losses this year. It had nothing to
do with losses. It was something else; I'm not sure what it was.*
1/7/93

I've never been a quitter and I've never been a guy to walk away
from a challenge, but the opportunity has to be the right opportunity
for me. It will have to be absolutely the right opportunity, and I will
have to be able to do everything I want to do with my people to make
it work. 1/7/93

REFLECTIONS ON HIS FIRING IN 1997

*I ceased to want to go to work. I didn't care about being around the
place. I had some people who didn't shoot straight with me. That
bothered me... It became so under-the-table.*
8/24/97 New Orleans Times-Picayune

Everybody was going in a different direction when I got there. We
got rid of all the power struggles, the egos and all that and just had
people playing football. We had a single-minded purpose, which
was to be a winner, to be a Super Bowl winner. When you looked at
what we accomplished there, I didn't deserve to go out that way.
8/24/97 *New Orleans Times-Picayune*

Ditka on Mike McCasky:
*I'm not mad at him. I was hurt in the beginning. Not to have been
hurt would have been silly. People can say anything they want to
say, but the record was pretty good. You just don't let a guy go because
one season goes down the drain. I became vulnerable. I made some
mistakes that created it. It hurt. But I understood it. I told him a
long time ago that I never wanted to coach there one minute past the
minute he didn't want me. I wish I would have known that [he didn't
want me coaching the Bears] earlier, in 1986.*
8/18/97 Chicago Sun-Times

THE FINAL THOUGHT

I'd never been vulnerable before. I'd always overcome it. I thought
I had actually got to a point where I was above that stuff. I was
wrong, dead wrong. I'll never let that happen again.
8/24/97 *New Orleans Times-Picayune*

NEW SAINTS COACH

A New Saints Era

I have softened. But don't push me.
2/2/97 New Orleans Times-Picayune

I think I'm supposed to be a coach, not a world traveler. I was a world traveler for four years and I enjoyed it. But I don't miss any of those things. I don't even think about them.
4/6/97 *Chicago Sun Times*

Diana Ditka on being "surprised anyone
had the balls to hire [her husband]:"
I'm very direct. First of all, I had no idea it would end up on national TV. But it's the truth. Mike's been available for years and no one hired him. I hope I don't offend any other team owners by saying that, but then again—who cares?
5/18/97 New Orleans Times Picayune

SAINTS OWNER, TOM BENSON

Tom Benson on his first meeting with Mike Ditka:
I promise you, I didn't know what to expect, and neither did Mike. I'm convinced he wasn't sure what he wanted to do. He came to San Antonio for one reason, to hear what we had to say, to find out how serious I was about putting a winning team on the field, a Super Bowl team. 8/1/97 *New Orleans Times-Picayune*

Ditka on first meeting Benson:
I told Tom Benson, "If you want somebody else, go get him." I said, "You know my qualifications, you know what I've done, and you have a pretty good idea of the way I'll run the ship." That's what he wanted. That's why I was elated over the opportunity. Once the opportunity was there, I realized the biggest thing I missed in life is the challenge of coaching, the challenge of working with players and trying to build an organization. That was the biggest fun of it in Chicago. It ceased being fun that last year.
8/24/97 New Orleans Times-Picayune

Tom Benson:
It's hard to explain, but something just clicked, I guess Mike liked what I was saying, too. He's a very upfront guy. He tells you exactly what's on his mind...I like that. Period.
8/1/97 New Orleans Times-Picayune

Tom Benson on Ditka's contract:
We have a hell of a deal. I just can't believe how he fell out of heaven to us. 1/29/97 New Orleans Times-Picayune

BREAKING THE CHICAGO TIES

I'm a Saint. Nothing else. I'm a Saint, through and through.
6/29/97 New Orleans Times-Picayune

Responding to a question about the Saints
playing the Bears in Chicago in a preseason game:
The Chicago thing, I'll never get personal about it. I got personal about going back against the Cowboys and playing the first game against Buddy [Ryan]. It's not personal. It has nothing to do with me and the Bears; it has to do with the players on the field. But it's going to be sentimental because I did it there a lot of years and because I have a lot of friends there. 4/6/97 *Chicago Sun Times*

Asked by a Chicago reporter what he missed about Chicago:
Not being able to see my kids as much. Friends I built up over that period of time that I sit around and play cards with, golf with. I miss my partners in the (restaurant) business. I knew saying goodbye to friends would be the hardest part. Chicago has been awfully good to me. It really has. It's a great city. It's amazing the fans still come up to La Crosse. They had the Bears stuff on and said they were rooting for the Saints second. I don't know why they drove all the way up to La Crosse. It's crazy. 8/18/97 Chicago Sun-Times

One thing I have to clarify. Now I'm a Saint. It kind of amazes me when people bring me the bubble-gum cards with me on the Bears. I'm a Saint. I really am. It's taken a little while. It took me longer to get the feeling here than when I went to Chicago, but I've got it totally now. 8/18/97 Chicago Sun-Times

CHICAGO'S REACTION

Mike North, Chicago sports personality, on the reaction in
Chicago to Ditka being hired to coach the Saints:
It's like the entire city received a blood transfusion. Ditka is dominating the conversation here.
2/2/97 New Orleans Times-Picayune

Chicago sports columnist Bob Verdi:
Mike was a great player here. He symbolized everything the Bears personified in Chicago. He is an original. He was rough, tough and

didn't take any B.S.... He was always emotional, and what you saw during the press conference was a kaleidoscope of the man's makeup. He got choked up, feisty, reflective. He wasn't nicknamed 'Sybil' by the Bears players for no reason. The bottom line on the attraction is, this town embraced that '85 team unlike any other, including the Bulls' championship teams. It will never forget it.
2/2/97 New Orleans Times-Picayune

THE NEW SAINTS COACH

There's going to be changes made. I think anybody that doesn't understand that would be a fool. We're going to make some changes, but the people who stay, I think, are enjoying it.
1/29/97 New Orleans Times-Picayune

I will tell you this from the bottom of my heart and I will say this on behalf of our coaching staff that the only kind of players that we'll keep are players who really want to play for the New Orleans Saints and who got out there and bust their [butt]. There is only one goal to have and you might as well say it, it's to win the Super Bowl.
4/8/97 New Orleans Times-Picayune

I want to create a sense of pride, a greater sense of pride in what this organization is all about. Some people say why, and I say why not? Why not us? Why can't we be the guys who do it? It's not going to come easy, but nothing good in life ever does come easy.
1/29/97 New Orleans Times-Picayune

Slogan for the 1997 Saints season:
We will find a way or we will make a way.
6/7/97 New Orleans Times-Picayune

Is it realistic to have a little toy cart moving around Mars picking up stones? Anything is realistic in life. If you don't dream big, then you're not going to have anything good happen. That's our goal... Anything can happen. 7/18/97 New Orleans Times-Picayune

There's only one goal in this league. You can soft-soap it. You can say: 'Well, we're going to improve. We're going to rebuild.' You can put all the words you want to put into it. But the bottom line is that we're going to win. That's what we have to do. We have to find a way to win. That's our motto. We have to find a way and make a way. That's the way it's going to be.
7/18/97 *New Orleans Times-Picayune*

THE SAINTS ORGANIZATION REACTION

New Orleans Saints General Manager Bill Kuharich on choosing Ditka as the head coach:
There was one [quality] that was most significant and made my decision very easy. He's a winner, and that's the bottom line. That's what we're in this business for: to win. Everything else is secondary.
1/29/97 New Orleans Times-Picayune

Bill Kuharich on his reasons for recommending Mike Ditka as the Saints head coach:
You need a leader, you need a Pied Piper. You need somebody to rally around. And Mike Ditka has those attibutes. You need a winner, a guy who has done it before as a player and a coach, and had been to a Super Bowl and won it. Mike Ditka has done that. You need a guy who is intense and passionate and would get guys to play.
11/27/97 New Orleans Times-Picayune

Greg Suit:
New Orleans loves its characters. New Orleans loves people who appear to be larger than life. It was kind of that way with [former Saints coaches] Hank Stram and Bum Phillips. But those people had not become a national celebrity on their way into this job, which Mike is. 8/24/97 *New Orleans Times-Picayune*

Saints defensive coordinator Zaven Yaralian:
From Mike Ditka, I learned the fire, the energy that Mike has. He's such a competitor, it's unbelievable. I've learned from him the competitive edge... 11/14/97 New Orleans Times-Picayune

Ditka on Yaralian:
When I sat Yaralian down, put him on the (black) board, I asked him what he'd do in these situations, what his philosophy was, I knew he was the guy I wanted. He's not a 'Yes' man
11/14/97 *New Orleans Times-Picayune*

Bobby April on being selected to stay with the Saints:
I'm elated Mike Ditka is going to be the coach. He does have a presence. I think this is great for this franchise. I'm very positive about this. 1/29/97 New Orleans Times-Picayune

Ditka on Bobby April:
I don't believe there's a better special teams coach in the country than Bobby. 1/29/97 *New Orleans Times-Picayune*

Abramowicz on Ditka:
...Players relate to him because he has played the game. He knows what it takes. He's firm, but he's fair. If you're honest and forthright with him, he'll be the same with you. But don't get on his (bad) side. 4/4/97 New Orleans Times-Picayune

Ditka on Danny Abramowicz:
Once you get into coaching and you have certain abilities, you can do many things. Danny has those abilities. He's a great teacher. He's a great innovator, and he knows football thoroughly.
8/24/97 *New Orleans Times-Picayune*

Saints assistant head coach/linebackers coach Ken Venturi:
You've got to be excited. We're starting a new era, and anytime you're part of that it's outstanding. Mike's presence is felt everywhere. I'm looking forward to the training camp. I think it's going to be unique, in his style. I think we're going to find out a lot about our team very quickly. 7/19/97 New Orleans Times-Picayune

GETTING THE SAINTS READY

FREE AGENCY AND THE SALARY CAP

On free agency:
It gets silly. This agent takes this guy to this team. He shops him with that team and says I can get this. I don't like that. I've played and been in this business too long. I don't like that when people do that. It's not meat on the hoof. I just think a player has to have some idea that he wants to go play for a team for more reason than whoever gives him the highest contract. 2/16/97 *New Orleans Times-Picayune*

On the Saints salary cap:
We're trying to free up money now. If we want to be stupid, we could free up $17 million (by making) wholesale cuts, and the money would be there. But that would cost us down the line. We're not going to do that. 3/13/97 New Orleans Times-Picayune

We may sign one or two [free agents] it depends. The key is, first of all, they have a deadline. If they want to be here, they'll be here. If they don't want to be here, that's fine. I don't want guys who figure they're going to miss a week of training camp and then they come in and we're going to fall over ourselves because they're here. If they were that good, they wouldn't be out there in the first place. 7/20/97 *New Orleans Times-Picayune*

I'm one of those coaches who's still in the Dark Ages. But I don't believe people who do nothing but block in the backfield are worth $2 million or whatever they think they're worth.
3/16/97 New Orleans Times-Picayune

Departing Saints

LORENZO NEAL

After signing with the New York Jets:
It was just a matter of getting a fresh start. There was some (bad feelings). Maybe if things would have been great, I would have never left. But I can't lie. It wasn't the perfect relationship. Yeah, they (the Saints) have new coaches and a new sheriff in town, and things could have been resolved. But it's still the same place, and I just made the decision to have new surroundings.
3/28/97 *New Orleans Times-Picayune*

Mike Ditka on Lorenzo Neal signing with the Jets:
I think what bothered him was he thought he was jerked around here in the past, and that's silly. Because the past is the past. We've all been jerked around in the past. But I can't control the past. I told him, 'You come here, wipe the slate clean, and you can be an integral part of this football team.' But I also told him, 'If you don't want to be here, then don't come. Don't waste your time, and don't waste my time. 3/28/97 New Orleans Times-Picayune

JIM EVERETT

We made a proposal that was unacceptable to Jim and his representative. If Jim wants to come back and play football this year, there is an open door. But there has got to be give and take on both sides. *4/1/97 New Orleans Times-Picayune*

Jim Everett:
I can tell you this: I plan on being here, and I plan on playing very well. I can't control what everybody else is saying. My frame of mind is to come in here and show Mike Ditka that I'm the quarterback. *4/27/97* New Orleans Times-Picayune

On terminating the contract of Jim Everett:
I thought it would be unfair to bring Jim back and put him through another quarterback school and a minicamp when I have intentions of going another way... If we drew this out and we let this go into training camp and August and then did it, we really severely disable his ability to go somewhere else. That's why I wanted to do it right now... It had nothing to do with Jim or his football ability at this point. It had to do with me being the head coach and the direction I want to take this football team. *5/16/97 New Orleans Times-Picayune*

Jim Everett:
It's not that I didn't anticipate it. I anticipated something like that in March or April. I didn't know they wanted to basically toy with me for that period of time. But the decision to get Heath was the right call. I just felt that I was being used for a point and being misled. *9/5/97* New Orleans Times-Picayune

RENALDO TURNBULL

On Renaldo Turnbull walking off the field after being criticized:
Anyone who does that is through with me. Why? Because he's not walking out on me; he's walking out on the team.
2/14/97 New Orleans Times-Picayune

On Renaldo Turnbull:
If he walks off the field on me, he'll never come back on the field for me. Unless there was a great explanation, like he had to go to the bathroom, you know. 3/13/97 New Orleans Times-Picayune

We have to find out about Renaldo. Renaldo is either going to do it, or he isn't going to do it. That's up to him. I can't make it happen. I want it to happen for his sake, but he's the only who can make it happen. If it happens, fine; if he doesn't, then we'll change that situation and go in another way. 6/1/97 *New Orleans Times-Picayune*

On Renaldo Turnbull missing three practices
as a result of an injured quadriceps muscle:

If [Turnbull] can't play through that kind of an injury, that's his problem. It's not mine. His teammates see that. I see and I wonder. I'm not blaming him; I'm just saying I wonder. I see a lot of guys out there today who could have said, "Well, I don't think I want to be out there today. It's hot and we're going against the Kansas City Chiefs," and this and that. But they're out there.
7/27/97 New Orleans Times-Picayune

Renaldo Turnbull:

If I'm not here, then I wish them all the best in the world, and that's the God's truth, because I have friends on this team. I think the coaching staff has come in and really worked hard to make it a winning organization. 8/13/97 *New Orleans Times-Picayune*

Renaldo Turnbull on being released:

The decision was in my court. They made me an offer. I turned it down because for me, football was something that should be fun. I was not having fun. I did not feel very comfortable with the situation I was being placed in. I thought it was in my best interest as well as my family's to make a break. At that point, once you sever those ties, you've got to move on. 10/16/97 New Orleans Times-Picayune

TORRANCE SMALL

Saint wide-receiver Torrance Small:

I expect it to be pretty tough with a new coach coming to a team. If it takes getting up in your face and weeding out who really cares and who doesn't want to be here, I don't see anything wrong with that. 4/4/97 *New Orleans Times-Picayune*

MICHAEL HAYNES

Ditka on his impression of the early workouts of Michael Haynes:
I like him. The only thing I told Michael after practices, we've got to get off the ball on the bump-and-run. Everything else, he catches the ball, he runs well. I'm not worried about the other thing, I'll get him to block. 4/8/97 New Orleans Times-Picayune

Michael Haynes on being released:
Mike [Ditka] told me he had decided he was going to go with the younger guys. He's just carrying out his plan.
5/29/97 New Orleans Times-Picayune

TERRY GUESS

On Terry Guess, wide receiver:
With Terry, it's very simple: It's time to take the kid gloves off and let him relate to life. He's not very focused on what his life is all about. I don't know if he wants to play football. He hasn't really acted like he does. He has a talent [speed] that you can't coach, and yet he doesn't seem to do a whole hell of a lot with it.
7/13/97 New Orleans Times-Picayune

When asked where Terry Guess failed to measure up:
Too many places. It's not even worth talking about. He's long gone.
8/19/97 New Orleans Times-Picayune

LEE DERAMUS

On Lee Deramus, wide receiver:
I like Lee a lot, but he's got to be more consistent in what he's doing, and he's got to stay healthy. The rap I heard on him is his hands. I don't think that's his problem. He might lose concentration, but he's got good enough hands. 7/13/97 New Orleans Times-Picayune

I think Lee can play in this league, I really do. I just don't know when it's going to happen for him. He's a big guy, and he's got to use his size and his strength to his advantage. He's got to become a mug out there. He's got to become a thug and beat people up and be physical and not let anybody take the ball away from him. But I like Lee DeRamus a lot. 8/19/97 *New Orleans Times-Picayune*

MARK MCMILLIAN

Mark McMillian on his demotion to back-up cornerback:
I have nothing against Alex [Molden]. He's a good ballplayer, and he's going to be a good ballplayer. But from the day I was brought in, it has been, 'You lose your job on the field.' I guess Ditka does it a different way. So I'm going to have to adjust to his style. He's the head coach, he makes the decisions. I don't know if it is a mind game or a motivating game, to put me down and put someone in front of me. Ditka doesn't really know me, and I don't know him. I came here thinking we were going to build on something that was the strong part of our team last year, then all of a sudden, it was like musical chairs. You've got to wonder that something's going on.
4/5/97 New Orleans Times-Picayune

EARNEST HUNTER

It was very hard with Earnest, because Earnest has played well. But we're in a situation now where he would be the fourth tailback, and we don't need that. We need somebody who can go in and block. 8/25/97 *New Orleans Times-Picayune*

DRAFT 1997

We need picks. We need more picks than we do one player. But yet if that one player is a guy who can step in and play for you for 10 years, take him, play him and don't even look back. Forget about other picks. 3/30/97 New Orleans Times-Picayune

On first round picks:
You've got to get them on the field and give them a chance to help your team immediately. All the guys I drafted at Chicago, except for Jim Harbaugh, who played later, played right away. If we pick 'em high, chances are you'll see them on the field. I'm not going to hide them. 3/30/97 *New Orleans Times-Picayune*

If you were to bet on one sure thing,(in the draft), it would have to be Orlando Pace. That's it. And sitting in second position, we had no guarantee that he would be there. Now I know what everybody is saying, 'The Jets are going defense.' I'm not sure that I buy all that. I read the book. There are a lot of smokescreens that happen [the Jets eventually traded the No.1 pick to Saint Louis]. 4/6/97 New Orleans Times-Picayune

Saints director of college scouting, Bruce Lemmerman:
We did the right thing for our football club when we made the trade (with Oakland). There was no guarantee the Pace would be there when we picked No.2. Based on what happened today, you have to like the way it turned out for us.
4/18/97 *New Orleans Times-Picayune*

After exchanging first round picks with the Oakland Raiders and cutting offensive guard Jim Dombrowski:
We look at this team right now as a jigsaw puzzle, and there's a couple of missing pieces. What we've tried to do is structure ourselves in the draft so that we can fill some of the jigsaw pieces. That's all. We think we can do that right now in the position we're in and pick some people that can be helpful to this football team in 1997.
4/1/97 New Orleans Times-Picayune

Before draft day on the possibility of making more trades:
There's a 70-30 chance we'll stay where we are. We need more picks. If you can end up with as many picks within the top 100 players, you can pretty much guarantee yourself of bringing in five or six people who have an excellent chance of making your football team.
4/19/97 *New Orleans Times-Picayune*

JARED TOMICH

**Nebraska defensive end Jared Tomich
on being drafted by the Saints:**
*I'm thrilled. I've been a huge Coach Ditka fan since I was a kid.
For me, it's kind of like a dream come true to get the chance to play
for him. 4/20/97* New Orleans Times-Picayune

ROB KELLY

He reminds me of a Gary Fencik a tremendous amount. He knew
what he was doing. He was smart, and used his talents to a maximum.
He knew how to blitz. He knew how to play the ball. He knew how
to come up and hit. Now his strength wasn't covering, which is
probably not Rob's strength. We're not asking him to cover that
much. 4/20/97 *New Orleans Times-Picayune*

Rob Kelly on Ditka:
*With Coach Ditka being a legend in coaching and in the NFL, to
hear him say that kind of stuff is just an amazing thing. But I know
I've got a lot to prove down there (in New Orleans). To be compared
to somebody like that already, I don't know if that's a really fair
comparison. But I'm definitely going to go down there and work my
butt off to contribute to the team.*
4/20/97 New Orleans Times-Picayune

CHRIS NAEOLE

On the Saints number one pick, Chris Naeole:
*He's a great football player in our mind. Chris is a great character
person. He's my kind of football player, first of all. He's a tough
guy. I think he's one guy I might be able to holler at and he wouldn't
get his feeling hurt too bad. 4/20/97* New Orleans Times-Picayune

TROY DAVIS

This kid is a big-time guy. He's not a small guy, he's short. He has the potential of staying on the field all three downs. He can be a spot guy, he can return kicks, he can do a lot of things.
4/20/97 New Orleans Times-Picayune

Troy Davis on Ditka:
[Ditka] said I was going to be the man, that I was going to touch the ball 30 times a game. I want to show I can be the man and help this team win. *4/20/97* New Orleans Times-Picayune

Troy Davis:
It's what I've got in my heart. I think I can go against anybody. It doesn't matter how small or how big you are. It's who wants it the most, and that's what I always dream about. I want it the most.
4/26/97 New Orleans Times-Picayune

DANNY WUERFFEL

Dan Reeves, head coach of the Atlanta Falcons, on the Saints pick of Danny Wuerffel ahead of the Falcons:
Obviously, Mike must see the same things in Danny that I do.
4/21/97 New Orleans Times-Picayune

On Danny Wuerffel:
I think the greatest criteria for evaluating people is what you've done. I don't know that you could evaluate anybody any other way than by what you've accomplished in life and what you've achieved. This guy's a winner, a true winner on every level he has played. I know you're going to hear all the so-called experts who'll say he can't, he can't and he can't. But you've got to look at all the cans. His strong points certainly outweigh anything that he doesn't do.
4/21/97 New Orleans Times-Picayune

On criticism of Danny Wuerffel's arm:
Did I see what all those experts saw? I must have missed it.
5/16/97 New Orleans Times-Picayune

Draft Evaluation & Training Camp

We know we are bringing in quality people who are going to go out and give you a full day's work for a full day's pay, and that's what I'm looking for. 4/20/97 *New Orleans Times-Picayune*

Asked his early impression of the rookies:
I think there's a lot to hang your hat on. I don't see anything that you can be discouraged about. You've got to realize I told these guys, 'Don't assume anything, and don't take anything for granted. But don't take anything off somebody.' I don't think they will. I think they understand. 4/27/97 New Orleans Times-Picayune

MINICAMP: ATTITUDE, CAMARADERIE, & CONDITIONING

Evaluating the Saints strength and conditioning:
We're not a strong football team. We intend to get our people in shape. Those that don't wish to be in shape won't be here. I'm not going to play with people who can't play in the fourth quarter, who are going to quit in the fourth quarter.
3/13/97 *New Orleans Times-Picayune*

We want to try and get an attitude and a camaraderie created on this football team. We see a little bit of it...down in the weight room. But I think we need more of it. We need more people respecting and understanding that they have to count on each other on the practice field and the playing field. 3/30/97 New Orleans Times-Picayune

Our job right now is to present our message to them, tell them who we are and what we're going to do. Those who want to be a part of it, fine. Those who don't, that's fine, too... So if they want to be a part of this and get on the bandwagon, then the price they're going to

pay is going to be told to them. This is not a slave labor camp. All we're trying to do is say if it was easy to win, everybody would win. Certain prices have to be paid...those that stick with us, they'll reap the benefits when it comes time.
3/30/97 *New Orleans Times-Picayune*

After the second minicamp:
Every day we got a little better, so the improvement is there. We've got a long way to go, and I'm not going to fool myself, I'm not going to fool [the players], and I'm not going to fool you. But we're going in the right direction. A lot of good things are happening—a lot of enthusiasm, a lot of hustle, a lot of effort. That's the main thing right now. We're building on it. 4/28/97 New Orleans Times-Picayune

I could tell you it's going to be all about brotherhood and being nice guys, but I'd be lying to you. I want my players to be tough guys. I want them to play tough, think tough, act tough. It's going to start from Day 1 at training camp—one on one. They're going to hate each other. But by hating each other to a degree, playing against each other at that tempo, that will make each other better.
7/17/97 *New Orleans Times-Picayune*

The goal of the Saints:
[It's] to win football games and earn the respect of the fans, the people in the community, the media by the way we play the game... We've got to find a way to be the toughest guy on the block. Once you're the toughest, you can [...] on a few people and get away with it. But we got to get tough. We got to find a way to do that.
7/17/97 New Orleans Times-Picayune

REGULAR TRAINING CAMP

Saints cornerback Eric Allen on camp:
It's been a lot calmer than I anticipated based on what I heard talking to a lot of ex-Bears. They warned me about all of this running we'd do. I was in the off season running my butt off, and it helped out. But Mike's been pretty calm...What he doesn't like is guys that are

maybe banged up who don't push it. You have to work and practice hard with Coach Ditka, and he'll give you that respect.
7/23/97 New Orleans Times-Picayune

Ditka on camp:
This is not boot camp. It's not meant to be a boot camp. It's not meant to get anybody beat up or tired any more than you have to.
7/23/97 New Orleans Times-Picayune

Wayne Martin on camp:
This is the most fun I've had in training camp since I've been playing. Everything is new that we're doing. New people. It just feels different. Coach Ditka has won big games. He's a legend. It's enjoyable playing for him... You come to work and do your job, play hard and practice hard, and you're a man.
7/23/97 New Orleans Times-Picayune

Heath Shuler on the way Ditka treats his players:
He doesn't want players to be someone they're not. He wants to see the real person, the person that's inside. You're going to get the most out of a player if they're going to be themselves. That's where you get your leadership role. The true leaders are going to step forward. They don't have to push themselves to be leaders. If they're not leaders, he wants them to be good followers.
7/23/97 New Orleans Times-Picayune

It's our job as coaches to get 'em ready to play football. It's there job as players to play football. This is not brain surgery. It's just football. It's a matter of wanting to do it bad enough to do it right.
8/1/97 New Orleans Times-Picayune

CURRENT SAINTS OFFENSIVE PLAYERS

The Saints Offense

HEALTH SHULER

Heath Shuler:

Mike being here made quite a bit of difference. I did want the opportunity to be a starting quarterback. But the next thing was obviously Mike. You want a guy that's going to be a leader. You want a general on the sidelines, and I don't think there's a better general in the game. 6/8/97 New Orleans Times-Picayune

Mike Ditka on the acquisition of Heath Shuler:

We filled our biggest need. We think that we'll have two No.1 draft picks. We (traded for) one in Heath, and we'll draft another one tomorrow. 4/19/97 *New Orleans Times-Picayune*

Heath Shuler:

This is a chance to revive myself, get back in the swing of things, and as Coach (Ditka) would say, put a smile on my face and go out and

171

have fun because that's the name of the game. All I ask of any team is, I want to go to a place that wants to win and be with an organization that you can get a chance. Today when I walked through the doors (of the Saints training facility), I knew this was the place, without question. 4/19/97 New Orleans Times-Picayune

Do I know what I'm doing? Well, we'll find out. But there are a lot of qualities I really like in Heath. There's a tough will, a tough mind, and I think there's a leader there. I've got a man on a mission. You can say it's bad, or you can say it's good, but he's on a mission now. I like people like that, because he's out to prove himself. Not necessarily to prove others wrong, but out to prove himself.
5/16/97 *New Orleans Times-Picayune*

Do I think Heath can do the job? I certainly do. If I didn't think Danny [Wuerffel] or Nuss [Doug Nussmeier] could do the job, they wouldn't be here. I can't afford to have a guy as backup who I don't feel confident in, who I don't think the team feels confident in, and put him in the game. That's silly. 7/13/97

After Saints fans booed Shuler in the Charger game
and yelled for rookie quarterback Danny Wuerffel:
There is no point in that now. Heath is the quarterback. This is not fun for me or the fans. I don't expect fans to condone the kind of offense we played. We have to have execution. I take responsibility.
9/8/97 *New Orleans Times-Picayune*

He's got to realize to play the game, you've got to take your steps, you've got to take your drops, you've got to take your reads and then you've got to execute. And it's not easy. I told him, "I don't think you believe in yourself as much as I believe in you."
10/9/97 New Orleans Times-Picayune

After replacing Shuler during the Atlanta game and naming
Danny Wuerffel as the starting quarterback for the next game:
It's not a matter that I'm totally unhappy with Heath. It's just that we need a spark right not. We need to find a way to win a football

game. We need a way to make some plays. And I don't know if Danny's the guy or not. We're going to find out. We're going to take a run at it. 10/14/97 New Orleans Times-Picayune

Shuler:
It's just part of the game. We'll see how things go. If I get another chance, get another opportunity to go back in, I'll have to make the best of it. There ain't much to say about it. I had to make plays, and unfortunately I didn't. [Ditka] had to do something, to change up the routine or something. That's what happens. That's part of the game, part of being a quarterback. I was given chances. A lot of times I didn't make the plays when they were there.
10/24/97 *New Orleans Times-Picayune*

MARIO BATES

Mario Bates:
If I'm given the ball consistently, I will do what the main back is supposed to do: Score 12, 13 touchdowns and run for 1,000 yards. I just have to stay healthy. 6/13/97 New Orleans Times-Picayune

I'm impressed with his attitude, the way he's practiced, the way he's run the football, the way he has tried to block, the way he's running. He's done everything we've asked. He's been great. He's not a great catcher of the ball, but he's catching the ball better. I'm tremendously impressed with what he's done so far. I've heard all the negative things. I haven't seen them. I've only seen the positives.
8/24/97 *New Orleans Times-Picayune*

On the demotion of running back Mario Bates:
Mario's got to take the responsibility of going out and playing good football. Nobody's going to baby him around here. Either he does it or he doesn't. I'm not going to worry about that.
9/6/97 New Orleans Times-Picayune

Mario Bates on the uncertainty of starting each game:
I actually don't even know what to say about it. It's just one of those

things. With Mike Ditka, you never know what's going to go on. One week it might be me. One week it might be Troy. Or just whatever he thinks is going to work that week. I prepare myself each week, every week. 11/8/97 New Orleans Times-Picayune

RAY ZELLARS

I want to prove that I'm a complete player as well as a team player and that I'm not selfish. I just want to win, and I'll do whatever it takes to win. 4/5/97 *New Orleans Times-Picayune*

Ray Zellars on his expectations:
I'm very upbeat about the season, very excited and looking to get better every day. I have big expectations for the team as well as myself. We're hungry. We have a taste of winning now, and I think the team likes it. Mike has brought a new attitude, a new air of excitement to the team. He's the type of coach that you want to play for... 8/15/97 New Orleans Times-Picayune

IRV SMITH

Irv is a starter until someone beats him out. Tony (Johnson) hasn't beaten him out. Until somebody beats him out, Irv is the starter. Our tight end has to do what the old tight ends did. He can't just run down the field and catch the ball. I don't care about that stuff. He's got to be an extension of the tackle. He's got to be able to hook a linebacker, and block a defensive end. He has to be another lineman that can catch the ball. 7/13/97 *New Orleans Times-Picayune.*

JOHN FARQUHAR

John has stepped up and played. The thing you've got to realize is there's not a lot of difference. Take them, throw them all up in the air and they land. They look alike. You don't see a guy for four weeks and you kind of forget what he did for you. I'm not knocking Irv (Smith, the Saints other tight end). I like Irv a lot. Irv was one of the guys who was going to be a cornerstone or our offense, and he still probably will be. But I'm saying that you've got to look at the reality of what is there. 10/4/97 New Orleans Times-Picayune

ANDRE HASTINGS

Free-agent Andre Hastings on the Saints:
I think they're looking for more production here. That's [the feeling] I got from Coach Ditka, the [offensive] coordinator, and the special teams coach. And they feel like I've been productive over my years in Pittsburgh. 3/21/97 *New Orleans Times-Picayune*

JERRY FONTENOT

I think the main thing is we got a guy to solidify our offensive line. This is a real tough guy. He does a lot of things you really can't teach. I think we can insert him into our lineup and better because of him. 4/20/97 New Orleans Times-Picayune

Jerry Fontenot:
He [Ditka] still motivates me. He's been there before. He's played and coached in the big games, and he's been very successful. Whatever I can learn from him today, as well as what I learned four years ago, I want to stick with me. He teaches principles that you can use in life; dedication, hard work and giving everything that you have to the game. He knows how to be successful. He can teach a lot of young guys on this team a lot of good things.
8/14/97 *New Orleans Times-Picayune*

ANDY McCOLLUM

All I do is look at films. He played awfully well at the center position. He really did. That's the key to me. That's not an easy position to play. But he's more adapted to moving. He was not reluctant to move, so there never was a problem. We watched him at guard before we even talked about doing the [Fontenot] deal. We thought Andy

could do it. I think it'll make us a better football team. I think Andy McCollum is a great football player.
6/7/97 *New Orleans Times-Picayune*

DARYL HOBBS

Wide receiver Daryl Hobbs, acquired from the Raiders:
Like Coach Ditka told me when I got here: 'Just work hard and everything will work itself out.' I couldn't ask for a better situation. This turned out to be the best situation for me.
6/8/97 New Orleans Times-Picayune

After an argument between Hobbs and offensive coordinator Danny Abramowicz, resulting in the release of Hobbs:
It's not a thing that's pleasant, and it's not a thing that should have happened. But when it does happen and it's not happening for the first, second or third time, then you've got to say, "Time out. Lets' get this thing in perspective. We run an organization this way, and that's the way we're going to run it, period. Cut and dried. We've said from day one, "Those who want to be here will be here. Those who don't, won't." If you don't want to be here, usually you'll display some acts that would leave the impression that you don't want to be around. 9/27/97 *New Orleans Times-Picayune*

CHRIS NAEOLE

Chris Naeole:
I'm very proud to be here [at camp] and be on time, and I'm ready to go to work. You know you've got Mike Ditka over here. You kind of feel pressure [to report to the camp on time]. Coach, he wants you in on time, and you can feel it. 7/17/97 New Orleans Times-Picayune

On Chris Naeole's injury, forcing him to miss 4 weeks:
Of all the drills for this to happen—with all the running and hitting that we do, it comes on a one-on-one drill. But this is part of football. You don't want this to happen, but it happens.
7/22/97 *New Orleans Times-Picayune*

He's way behind. There's no question about it. He's way behind in the sense that the preseason games would have really helped him. Playing against that quality of people and seeing different things, it would have helped him... Now it's going to be wait and see.
8/9/97 New Orleans Times-Picayune

TROY DAVIS

You've got to go back and look at the people who've gained 2,000 yards in the Big 12. There's not too many of them. One who has [Barry Sanders] is doing pretty good in Detroit. Another one [Thurman Thomas] had a great career in Buffalo. I think Troy can be in that same vein. Troy is there [to be tackled] and then he's not there. He's a pretty special runner. He went in there with no blocking one time, and he came out of the other side, and the guy wondered where he went. He'll make some people miss over time.
7/20/97 *New Orleans Times-Picayune*

Troy Davis:
I'm Troy Davis, and I'm the kind of cat that wants to run the ball. Mike Ditka's style is to run the ball, and if they give me the ball, I'm going to try to run my hardest with it. First, I've got to make the team. If I make the team, I want to start, and I feel I have a chance to be one of the starters. I'm going to try my best to be a starter.
7/20/97 New Orleans Times-Picayune

All you've got to do is watch. He's willing. He blocks. He probably blocks as well as anybody out there. He has no fear of anything, and he has a great will. He's trying to be something special. He really already is, but he's trying to be something maybe a little more than special. 7/20/97 *New Orleans Times-Picayune*

Davis:
Ditka sees a lot of potential in me. He knows that I can carry the team if I want to. But I just have to stop all these mental mistakes, like fumbling the ball... I think I can be like another Barry Sanders or Emmitt Smith. 9/11/97 New Orleans Times-Picayune

DANNY WUERFFEL

He has great vision. He has great command. He understands the offense as well as any of those guys right now. And when he doesn't he asks the questions. Sometimes the questions he asks makes us think about something we're doing.
7/22/97 *New Orleans Times-Picayune*

I don't think there's a guy coming out of college at that position ready to play more now than Danny Wuerffel because of the system he played in, the coaching he had under Steve [Spurrier] and the way he handles it. Nothing bothers this guy. You wouldn't know if he threw a touchdown, an interception. There's no show. Nothing bothers him. He's just going to come back the next play and do the best he can. That's the way he handles himself. He's very smart about running an offense. He sees things, and he feels things. [Jim] McMahon was that way a lot. He always knew what he had to do.
8/8/97 New Orleans Times-Picayune

On moving Wuerffel up from the number 3 quarterback to the number 2 quarterback:
This is no slap at Doug [Nussmeier]. They're both awfully close. We're probably going to have to use them both before it's over... If you watched the way he handled the offense [against Oakland], he has a pretty good grasp on things. Very few people could have run that offense like he did, under the pressure he was under, with the different defenses and looks they gave him. And to be able to audible to the amount of plays was pretty impressive.
8/19/97 *New Orleans Times-Picayune*

Anybody that doesn't like Wuerffel doesn't know football. He's not pretty, but he'll get it done. He's smart. What he doesn't know, he asks about. And there's not a whole lot he has to ask about.
8/21/97 New Orleans Times-Picayune

Nothing bothers him. Adversity doesn't bother him. Success doesn't bother him. He handles everything the same. You wouldn't know if he threw a touchdown or an interception. I think that's good.
10/18/97 *New Orleans Times-Picayune*

Danny Wuerffel on becoming the starting quarterback:

A few weeks ago, things were going bad, and I got in the game [against Atlanta], and people started playing a little better. So [Ditka] thought, "Why not give it a shot and see if everybody plays better and rallies around him?" It didn't work. It didn't work out for us. Now he's trying something different. I'm definitely supportive of that.
10/31/97 New Orleans Times-Picayune

DOUG NUSSMEIER

Doug Nussmeier on the quarterback competition:

In this league, you compete every day for your job. They [coaches] obviously made Heath a clear-cut starter. But I believe that I can play, and I believe I can be a starter for this team. It's just a matter of where everybody ends up. They've proclaimed Heath the guy, and I'm fine with that. But I believe I can play. It's a sad thing, but sometimes in order to get an opportunity somebody's got to go down, or something's got to happen. And that's hard to say, because I really like Heath, and he's a great guy.
8/12/97 *New Orleans Times-Picayune*

On Doug Nussmeier:

I'm not averse to putting Nuss in the game at any point. It doesn't bother me one bit, believe me. I think Nuss has practiced very well. I think he is much more accurate throwing the ball than I've ever seen him. I think his decision-making is outstanding in practice. I think he's got as good a command of the offense as anybody else - the plays, the formations, everything. I believe that he can go out and play. And I believe he'd play pretty darn well right now... I've been watching him pretty well for the last eight weeks, and his improvement has been significant. 10/14/97 New Orleans Times-Picayune

NICKY SAVOIE

On Nicky Savoie's sternum bruise:
I've had it. I know what it is. It's as painful as heck, but that's life.
There's nothing broken there. You put a pad on it, you take an aspirin,
and you go like heck. He's in the process of trying to make this
football team. 7/27/97 *New Orleans Times-Picayune*

Nicky Savoie's response:
*I heard what he said and it got to me. I said, "Why should Ditka be
tougher than me?"* 7/27/97 New Orleans Times-Picayune

DONALD WILLIS

Willis on his opportunity to be starter:
If somebody said to me, "I'm going to give you a chance to start in
the NFL, "whew, they would have to shoot me to get me out of that
guard position. 8/20/97 *New Orleans Times-Picayune*

DEREK BROWN

Tailback Derek Brown on Ditka:
It seems like we have a new organization here—a new staff, new
coaches, new players. We have a lot of young guys who are ready to
play. With the attitude and enthusiasm that Mike Ditka has brought
here, we're just ready to get started.
7/17/97 *New Orleans Times-Picayune*

After placing Brown on injured reserve for the entire season:
*As much as I like Derek Brown and as much as I want him on this
football team, you can't do it. He's a hell of a kid, the best conditioned
athlete on this team. I really respect him. But we just can't wait [for
Brown to get healthy]. This is a brutal business.*
8/26/97 New Orleans Times-Picayune

Derek Brown:
I was really looking forward to playing for Coach Ditka this season, because he gave me another chance. That's all I ever asked. The man has been so successful. It's an honor just to be able to say I made this team. But this is just a minor setback. I'm going to rehab, work hard during the offseason, and I'll be back next year. I'm going to stay positive. There isn't anything I can do about it. It happened and I've got to deal with it. 8/26/97 *New Orleans Times-Picayune*

RANDAL HILL

Hill on Ditka, Shula, and Jimmy Johnson:
Mike Ditka and Don Shula are very comparable. Both of them are very knowledgeable, specifically about the offense and defensive schemes. Both of them work hands on, offensively and defensively. Both of them come at you directly. Both of them look at you in your eyes and tell you exactly what they think of you. Jimmy Johnson is a little bit different. He's a little bit more of a talker. He's a little bit more of a motivator. But each one of these guys has been successful, and each one of these guys has the [Super Bowl] ring on their finger. So you can't knock any one of them.
8/7/97 New Orleans Times-Picayune

WILLIE ROAF

On Willie Roaf making the Pro Bowl:
I think Willie Roaf is an All-Pro; I really do. I think that anybody can have a bad game, and I think that's what probably happened to him (in the first Atlanta game) more than anything. Priorities, he's got to continue to work if he wants to keep that level of excellence. People are getting better in the league. I'm glad to see him make it, because I think he deserves it.
12/13/97 *New Orleans Times-Picayune*

BILLY JOE HOBERT

After acquiring Billy Joe Hobert from Buffalo:
He'll get in a foxhole and fight with you. I like that in people. He's tough. In Buffalo, we talked to [Bills executive vice president] John Butler up there. When he went up there originally, he probably thought he was going to be the starting quarterback. When it didn't work out that way, probably he didn't put in the application in that he should have. I don't see any problem with that right here.
11/20/97 New Orleans Times-Picayune

Billy Joe Hobert:
I'm as happy as hell. Five weeks ago I was driving a U-Haul from Buffalo to Seattle. That was the loneliest 42 hours I've ever had in my life. It gave me a lot of time to reflect. Truthfully, I thought I'd never have this chance again. 11/25/97 *New Orleans Times-Picayune*

**On Billy Joe Hobert going into the 1998
season as the number one Saints quarterback:**
I think that somebody would have to take the job away from him right now, and I don't think I'm saying anything unfair.
12/16/97 New Orleans Times-Picayune

ALVIN HARPER

**Two days after signing Alvin Harper
he sustained a sprained knee ligament:**
I know he's in a lot of pain right now. He can't move the knee. He would be very fortunate to be able to get back on the field. I don't see any way myself, but I'm not a doctor.
12/6/97 New Orleans Times-Picayune

CURRENT SAINTS
DEFENSIVE PLAYERS

The Saints Defense

On defense We've got to try some things. With Turnbull and Mark Fields (at weak-side linebacker), we know what their strengths are, and we've got to utilize their strengths, not their weaknesses. Their strengths are coming (applying pressure). We've got to be very aggressive. We've got to get faster. We know that. We need a nose tackle. We need a safety, we know that. I don't feel bad about our corners, and I don't feel bad about a lot of other things. Our ends and our tackle are very good football players.
2/16/97 New Orleans Times-Picayune

The defensive line:
We're still looking for a guy. We think we need one more guy. Whether he comes later, I don't know. I want a guy who is going to come in here and be part of the team. I'm not necessarily looking to get older unless I get better... But I want a guy who is going to practice every day. We're talking about doing some other things in the way

of eight man fronts. We want to stop the run and force them to pass. We're going to go after the quarterback. We're not going to sit back there and let them throw the ball. If we can't get there with four, we'll bring five. If we can't get there with five, we'll bring six. But we'll get there. 7/13/97 *New Orleans Times-Picayune.*

MARK FIELDS

I thought Wilbur Marshall could run... This guy is a really good football player. Everything is ahead of him. L.T. [Lawrence Taylor] in his best day didn't run like this kid runs. I don't think I've ever seen a linebacker run like this kid. He can be awfully special. A lot of it will be determined by how we use him...[to] maximize his talents where we can. I think we're going to do that. We're going to try to do it, anyway. 7/22/97 New Orleans Times-Picayune

ANTHONY NEWMAN

Right now, Anthony Newman is our starting strong safety. Right now, he is. 7/13/97 *New Orleans Times-Picayune*

WILLIE BROUGHTON

Truth is, I don't know what Willie can do. I got too many guys busting their...every day trying to be a part of the football team. I understand injuries happen. But when the injury is there for a long time, then why should I give it a chance to happen again? Let me correct that situation and put in a fresh body and go forward.
7/13/97 New Orleans Times-Picayune

JE'ROD CHERRY, ALEX MOLDEN AND ERIC ALLEN

On Je'rod Cherry and Alex Molden:
They're going to play. They're not here to watch. We saw enough of the guys who played. We got to get better. These are our people, and

if we're not going to give them a chance to make us better first, who the hell are we going to give it to. I think we've got to get Cherry on the field. We've got to find out about him. I think we've got to get better at the safety position as I see it right now. If Cherry was picked where he was picked in the second round, put him on the field and play him. If he can't play, then eat your mistake. Molden is going to the left corner position. For the time being that's where he'll play. Our safeties are not going to switch. They're going to have to play strong and free both. But we think [Cherry] would be more of a strong safety than a weak safety.
2/16/97 *New Orleans Times-Picayune*

On the competition at the Saint cornerback position between Mark McMillian, Alex Molden, and Eric Allen:

The two best will stay, the other one will leave.
4/4/97 New Orleans Times-Picayune

On Alex Molden:

He was drafted No. 1 last year, and we're going to give him a chance to be the starter... Now if he's not the best player, he won't start.
4/4/97 *New Orleans Times-Picayune*

WINFRED TUBBS

The more film I look at on Winfred, the more I think he's a pretty good football player. 2/18/97 New Orleans Times-Picayune

Ditka's advice to Tubbs:

You have got to learn that you can't play [middle linebacker] like Sam Mills. You've got to play like Jack Lambert, Dick Butkus or Ray Nitschke. You've got to be a mauler. You've got to be a Bear type. You don't have to be able to get under people and jack them up. You don't have to be this beautiful form tackler, either. Who cares? Just rip [a player's] head off and shove it down his neck every once in a while. 9/9/97 *New Orleans Times-Picayune*

Tubbs:
I think that comment did more for me than any other comment I've heard made toward me. 9/9/97 New Orleans Times-Picayune

RICHARD HARVEY

Saint linebacker Richard Harvey:
I'm not in a position to be protesting [participating in minicamp, even though NFL rules say that are not required to do so], I've got to come here and prove myself just like everybody else. And I want to do that. Everybody has to come in here and show what they can do. To be honest, we could have used more attitudes like that last year. 3/30/97 *New Orleans Times-Picayune*

Harvey:
If anyone is intimidated or leery of what's to come, then they don't need to be here. This is all about winning football games and preparing yourself to do that. To be honest, the media has done more with the whole Mike Ditka persona than anything else. The man is a head football coach. I don't think he's going to come in here and do anything that hasn't been done before. He's not going to rewrite the book. We're going to play football. But we are going to play a certain way, a certain style of football. We need to do that. We haven't done that, obviously. We were 3-13. 4/4/97 New Orleans Times-Picayune

MICKEY WASHINGTON

Veteran cornerback Mickey Washington on signing with the Saints: [Ditka] is a straight-forward person, and in this profession I think everyone can appreciate that. 6/3/97 *New Orleans Times-Picayune*

WAYNE MARTIN

Saints defensive tackle Wayne Martin:
The wealth in the NFL is so spread around. It [going to the Super Bowl] can be done. Mike Ditka has done it. The man has done it.

And if we get guys who are willing to do whatever it takes, than we can do it, too. 7/17/97 New Orleans Times-Picayune

Martin on Ditka:
You know he's successful, so it's easy for players to buy into what he's saying. Just his presence here, his mind-set is so different (from that of past coaching staffs). We have to keep working. He always tells us that Rome wasn't built in a day. Everything is new here this year. We're not going to be so quick to give up on things.
9/17/97 *New Orleans Times-Picayune*

VASHONE ADAMS

Vashone is not a guy that fell out of a tree. He started in the league and played pretty good...our coaches liked him a lot. I think he plays with a lot of enthusiasm on the field.
7/19/97 New Orleans Times-Picayune

On cutting Vashone Adams:
Everything is an attitude in life. How you handle it. Being put down is no big deal. But how you handle being put down, he didn't handle it very well. 10/2/97 *New Orleans Times-Picayune*

JARED TOMICH

Jared Tomich is going to be a good football player. When you look at Jared, he weighs 275. He looks like a little kid out there. He's not tall. So you think here's a small guy. But put 275 on a guy at end that can move like he can...that's a pretty good package.
7/30/97 New Orleans Times-Picayune

RICKEY JACKSON

Rickey is not a young man anymore, and he's been away from [the game] for a long time. The main thing I would be afraid of would be an injury. That would be the biggest thing. Sometimes what happens

when you get older as a football player, the mind is willing and the body is not capable. That's what happens. We all went through it. You say "I can do that." Then you look at the film and you say, "No, I can't do that anymore." You get a pretty good idea of how much you digressed. I saw that in my last year, believe me. Things you used to do easy you can't do anymore.
7/29/97 *New Orleans Times-Picayune*

Rickey Jackson:
I'm still on of the best [linebackers] in the world. I ain't lost nothing. If the right opportunity came along, you never know what would happen. But I'm not the type of guy to intrude... Mike makes all of the calls around here. I'm not trying to intrude into his show... If a guy like me wanted to play, why wouldn't he want to play for Ditka, a guy who likes tough, hard-nosed football players? I would like to play for Ditka. 7/29/97 New Orleans Times-Picayune

After announcing his retirement:
I was sluggish. My quickness just wasn't there...I proved to myself that I can still play, but I'm not the old Rickey Jackson that I used to be. I'm still good, and I can get out there and I still can play. But I'm not as good as I used to be. I can see that. My decision to retire is the best thing for me to do. 8/25/97 *New Orleans Times-Picayune*

SAMMY KNIGHT

Sammy Knight, you'd have to run him off with a big stick. I don't have a big stick. 8/6/97 New Orleans Times-Picayune

He's a sure tackler. I think when he gets his shots, he'll hit you as hard as anybody. But the main thing is, if you watch him, he's not a guy that misses tackles. He prides himself on his tackling.
8/6/97 *New Orleans Times-Picayune*

After the Saints 13-10 victory over the Raiders:
Sammy played great. He's going to make some rookie mistakes, but I remember reading something Sammy said about himself. He said, "I'm a good tackler, but not only am I a good tackler, I'm a sure tackler.' There's a lot of difference. Some guys can tackle, but they're not going to make all the tackles. Sam doesn't miss very many. He missed a couple in a couple of games, but I thought his open-field tackling was outstanding. He made one bad play on a route to [Raiders wide receiver Tim] Brown. But Sammy is not playing like a rookie at all. He's getting better and better.
11/12/97 New Orleans Times-Picayune

LA'ROI GLOVER

After acquiring defensive tackle La'Roi Glover from the Raiders:
He's not a real big guy. But he does some pretty interesting things. He gets his body in between people and ties people up pretty good. He's got some pass-rushing talent. He's a good kid. I like him. He'll help us. 8/28/97 *New Orleans Times-Picayune*

La'Roi Glover:
I'd rather not comment on what happened in Oakland. Things didn't work out for me there. But this is a great opportunity here. I am fortunate to be picked up by the Saints. They have high expectations here and that's great. Mike Ditka has brought a lot of enthusiasm to the team. They have a blue-collar attitude. This is going to be a good fit for me. 8/28/97 New Orleans Times-Picayune

ROB KELLY

On a mistake Rob Kelly made in the Raiders game:
...if you tell a free safety in three-deep coverage, "What's your responsibility?" He'll say, "Deep." But you can't carry it to the degree of backing out of the stadium. We're not going to flog him for missing a couple of plays. 11/12/97 *New Orleans Times-Picayune*

Rob Kelly:

I've had coaches get animated at me lots of times. I think it's tough to judge somebody on two or three plays. I've been chewed out many times for doing stuff, and I'm a big man. This is the NFL. You take it and move on and you learn from the situation... I've put that way behind me. I don't even think about that anymore. I'm just thinking about this being my opportunity to step up and play the kind of football I know how to play. And that's hard and aggressive, the type of football that Mike Ditka drafted me to 33rd to play. I've been waiting all year. 12/11/97 New Orleans Times-Picayune

CHRIS HEWITT

Chris Hewitt is on this football team because of the way he practices. I believe the guys we have on our practice squad are the guys I want to give the first chance to play.

11/17/97 *New Orleans Times-Picayune*

THE 1997 SEASON

Rams 38	Saints 24
Chargers 20	Saints 6
49ers 33	Saints 7
Saints 35	Lions 17
N.Y. Giants 14	Saints 9
Saints 20	Bears 17
Falcons 23	Saints 17
Panthers 13	Saints 0
49ers 23	Saints 0
Saints 13	Raiders 10
Saints 20	Seahawks 17 (ot)
Falcons 20	Saints 3
Saints 16	Panthers 13
Rams 34	Saints 27
Saints 27	Cardinals 10
Chiefs 25	Saints 13

RAMS 38 SAINTS 24
Rams Head Coach, Dick Vermeil:
If the game came down between Mike Ditka and I playing a football game, he'd win. He played in the NFL and he's in the Hall of Fame. I struggled being the starting quarterback at San Jose State my senior year, and I went into high school coaching. So he'd win going away.
8/31/97 New Orleans Times-Picayune

Howie Long, football analyst for the Fox network:
Because Vermeil and Ditka both are football coaches. First and foremost, that's what they are. Vermeil, I don't think, was ever content with the way his career ended. Ditka had a nice life working for NBC, but I think after a while he wasn't satisfied. They are doing what brings them happiness. I'm not sure they ever factored in the cost of failure, and that's something the media just doesn't understand. 8/31/97 *New Orleans Times-Picayune*

That was an old-fashioned butt-kicking.
9/1/97 New Orleans Times-Picayune

I wouldn't bet that could happen in a million years, that anybody would handle us like that on defense. Offensively, we were completely in a daze half the time. Once things didn't work the way we wanted them to work, we kind of got flustered. We kind of hit a brick wall, really. 9/1/97 *New Orleans Times-Picayune*

Heath is banged up pretty good, and I didn't want him to take any more punishment. Not that I wanted Danny to take it. I didn't want anybody to take it. But I thought it was time to get [Shuler] out of there. He's a pretty tough cookie.
9/1/97 New Orleans Times-Picayune

Heath Shuler:
Mike told me, "I'm not pulling you for the way you played. I'm pulling you before you get yourself killed."
9/1/97 *New Orleans Times-Picayune*

CHARGERS 20, SAINTS 6
Bill Kuharich, president and general manager of the Saints:
We need to run the ball more. Certainly, [Saints coach] Mike [Ditka] will address that situation because of his liking to run the football... I think you'll see us go back to that this coming game against the (San Diego) Chargers. 9/3/97 New Orleans Times-Picayune

San Diego Chargers quarterback Jim Everett on the game:
I don't think I could write a better script. It will be the first home
game for the Saints under "Da Coach." I know they'll be pumped
up, and I know I'll be pumped. I feel very emotional about this game.
I expect to play at a high level and I know they will, too. Some
things mean a lot to a person. This does to me.
9/5/97 *New Orleans Times-Picayune*

Jim Everett after putting the game out of reach
with touchdown pass with two minutes left in the game:
Someone asked me to write the script for this game. Well, it was
written with an exclamation point on the end with the last touchdown.
I don't think it could have happened any better.
9/8/97 New Orleans Times-Picayune

Promises are empty words if you're not keeping them. And right
now we haven't been able to keep them. And that bothers me.
9/11/97 *New Orleans Times-Picayune*

At Monday press conference with bloodshot eyes:
It's become very frustrating, so the hardest thing for me right now is
to sleep. 9/9/907 New Orleans Times-Picayune

49ERS 33, SAINTS 7
We're looking at trying to make the offense less vulnerable to mistakes
where...if the play doesn't go right, it's still not going to be a
catastrophe. Right now we're having catastrophes.
9/14/97 *New Orleans Times-Picayune*

HALFTIME BLOW-UP

Cornerback Eric Allen on reports that at halftime Ditka blew
up at the team and that Ditka and Allen had to be separated:
It's not constructive to talk about it, man. It was something that
happened at halftime and we want to leave it in the locker room. I
think I acted appropriately and hopefully it will pass. Mike has a

passion for the game. He displays it differently than other people. I know we didn't play well. I just think it was something he tried to do to motivate the team. 9/19/97 *New Orleans Times Picayune*

Anonymous player:
I've seen some wild things before but never anything like this. I hope this doesn't become the norm around here.
9/19/97 New Orleans Times-Picayune

Saints linebacker Mark Fields:
I don't think this dispels the myth that Mike has mellowed. I think he has some. I don't know if this was vintage Ditka because I haven't been around him long enough. I know this: I've seem Jim Mora's tirades and I think his were a little worse than Ditka's. Absolutely. But Mike's was a good one now.
9/19/97 *New Orleans Times-Picayune*

Ditka to the media on the incident:
I believe what happens in the locker room is meant to be in the locker room. Let me clarify it so you'll understand where I'm coming from. If I were to give them praise, that wouldn't be good news. That wouldn't be newsworthy, would it? If I were to praise them after the game, tell them how proud I am of them and really appreciate their effort and everything they're doing, nobody would write about that. I do that all the time. Nobody writes about that. So what you're trying to do is, you're looking at a negative factor which really wasn't a negative factor anyway. I just think it's easy to dwell on the negative things of life. But I'm not that way. I'm positive. Even when I was in the media [four years with NBC-TV], I wasn't negative. I just believe our society is too negative as it is.
9/20/97 New Orleans Times-Picayune

We just about handed them the football game in the first eight minutes. I'm not blaming Heath. I'm not going to sit here and crucify one guy. This is a team effort—players, coaches, everybody. Right now,

none of us are doing a very good job, and I put myself at the top of that list. We have to sit down and look at ourselves. All of us have to do a self-examination. We can all sit back and fool ourselves and say, "Well, I'm doing my job." But are you really? Who knows if we're all doing what we can do. We got to find that out.
9/15/97 *New Orleans Times-Picayune*

I'm not gonna quit. 9/15/97 New Orleans Times-Picayune

REGROUPING AFTER AN 0-3 START

I just told them [the team] we have to stay together. The only people that are going to help us is ourselves. We can't worry about what other people say or think because they're going to think and say what they want to. We have to do what we have to do to win a football game. That's all we can think about. We can't think about anything else. We can't think about down the road, what we're going to do for Thanksgiving or Christmas. We've got to think about Detroit and winning a football game. 9/17/97 *New Orleans Times-Picayune*

On the effects of an 0-3 start:
Oh-h-h, I'm 67 now. [He's 57]. 9/20/97 New Orleans Times-Picayune

THE QUARTERBACK CONTROVERSY

On starting Shuler or Wuerffel:
I'll be honest with you: I'm more worried about the team's psyche right now, and I'm trying to do the right thing for this football team to give us the best opportunity and chance to win. Because Heath does or doesn't start one week, doesn't mean that he'll start or not start the next week. I think we've got to take this as a game-to-game situation and see where the heck we're going. We've got to win a football game, gang. I would start anybody at quarterback to win a football game if I knew I could win a football game. That's the way I feel... 9/16/97 New Orleans Times-Picayune

This is not about me proving my decision was right to bring him here. I just believe he has the talent. I don't care about what people think. I want to make sure I don't pull the rug out from under him before it's time. 9/18/97 *New Orleans Times-Picayune*

The quarterback has to be the toughest guy on the team, mentally and physically. Look, I didn't anoint the quarterback position. People around the league and around the country have anointed the quarterback as somebody that, "You don't mess with his psyche." But I also have learned that quarterbacks aren't interchangeable parts, that one is as good as the other. I don't believe that anymore. 9/19/97 New Orleans Times-Picayune

SAINTS 35, LIONS 17
The main thing I want to clarify is if you think last week's halftime speech was something, this week's was unbelievable.
9/22/97 *New Orleans Times-Picayune*

You'll have to pardon me for laughing, but that monkey just got off my back, thank God. 9/22/97 New Orleans Times-Picayune

You've got to be realistic. It's only one game. We've had three weeks that were ugly, and we had one week that was kind of nice. Now we go to New York. And we'll find out more about this football team every week. I don't want to be too optimistic or too pessimistic. But I'm a realist. I know one thing, that if we play error-free football, we're going to create some problems for some people.
9/23/97 *New Orleans Times-Picayune*

GIANTS 14, SAINTS 9
I think you're looking at two football teams that are pretty much even right now. We're probably both trying to find out who we are. I think there are a lot of teams in this league right now after four games who don't know who they are. And some of those have winning records. You take the first three games and you throw them out and you judge everything on the fourth game, and yeah, we look like a

decent football team. You base it on the first four games (overall), and we're far down in the pack. There's no question about it. 9/28/ 97 New Orleans Times-Picayune

We are wandering through the desert looking for ourselves. We don't know who the hell we are. Not even close.
9/29/97 *New Orleans Times-Picayune*

We're 1-4 gang. Let's not fool ourselves. Nobody has sympathy for us, and they shouldn't. You play the kind of football we played today... I'm not proud of it. I'm not proud that we can't execute better than that in every area. You can sugar-coat it any way you want to, but right now we're not very good.
9/29/97 New Orleans Times-Picayune

Maybe I just overestimated how well we were going to do. I'm not going to talk about the talent. I think we have enough talent to win with. Does it always play up to my expectations? No, it doesn't. But that's part of life, that's part of coaching. I'm not going to knock them. I'm just going to say that I thought we'd be better, we aren't that good, and now I understand it's going to be a dogfight.
9/30/97 *New Orleans Times-Picayune*

After the loss to the Giants, Ditka at Monday's news conference:
I am tired. I'm emotionally tired. you can handle the physical aspects of it. The emotional aspects, it makes you tired. It makes you old. If you don't care, it doesn't matter. Unfortunately, I happen to care a lot. 10/1/97 New Orleans Times-Picayune

DAVE BROWN, GIANTS QB, RIPS DITKA

Dave Brown, New York Giants quarterback, on Ditka:
He's just another ex-Dallas assistant coach who thinks he knows it all. He's like a lot of the older coaches in the league now that aren't winning any games. A bunch of know-it-alls. Look at their record. They sit and criticize me—what have they done lately?
9/30/97 *New Orleans Times-Picayune*

Brown after a second touchdown:
That was for [Ditka]. He's dogged me long enough. He sat up there and criticized me when he didn't know any of the circumstances.
9/30/97 New Orleans Times-Picayune

Ditka's reaction:
He's right, what can I say? Dave Brown - when he's inducted into the Hall of Fame? Not to be critical of Dave Brown, [but] he's a very average football player that we made look better than he was. So what am I going to say? I'm going to say he's a great football player? I guess he's slapping Reeves and I when he says that [about ex-Dallas assistants]. But he'll be hard-pressed to win very much either with his talent. I criticized him royally [at NBC] because he deserved it. He was the reason that Dan is now in Atlanta - terrible football player last year. But let's leave it at that. He fired on me; I fired on him; we're even. 9/20/97 *New Orleans Times-Picayune*

SAINTS 20, BEARS 17
Diana Ditka's comments to Chicago Bears fans:
Nobody is going to win with that team as long as McCaskey owns it. They should be putting pressure on McCaskey, not Dave Wannstedt. Put pressure on McCaskey to sell it [the team]. 10/3/97

Offensively, we're still struggling. The Bears made us look pretty stupid at times but they [the Saints players] hung in there. They could have thrown in the towel. Earlier in the year, when the Bears went ahead, we would have said, "That's it. We're outta here." But they hung in there, and I'm proud of them."
10/6/97 New Orleans Times-Picayune

Our defense, you've got to love them:
We gave up some plays, but one (touchdown) drive was 8 yards and another was 33. Our defense, we're getting better. If this keeps up, and we get some people healthy, we're gonna be pretty good.
10/6/97 New Orleans Times-Picayune

Jerry Fontenot, ex-Bear now a Saint:
This week, he said he was going back to some of the old speeches he had stored... I'm sure it was a big game for Mike. I know it because he was very happy after the game. 10/6/97

I'll tell you what, I fell in love with these guys. I'm a sucker for that stuff. They're trying, and I know we aren't that good. But we're trying. If we could quit shooting ourselves in the foot, we could be competitive with people. We had three turnovers, they had none and we still win a football game. It's hard to believe. 10/6/97

FALCONS 23, SAINTS 17
I am not going to beat around the bush. Our job is to find a remedy. I made all of these mottos: Find a way, make a way. We better make a way, because we certainly haven't found one.
10/13/97 *New Orleans Times-Picayune*

After the loss:
We're [the coaches and the team] going to talk about a few things. But where are you going to change to? That's the question. We've gone through all of this before.
10/14/97 New Orleans Times-Picayune

PANTHERS 13, SAINTS 0

Well, we have hit bottom. Maybe we can bounce back. I don't know. I would like to apologize about the way we are playing. It is not very good. I expect people to be hard on us and beat us up, because we deserve it. All of us. Players, coaches, everybody. We're as bad as I've seen on offense, and I'm going back a long time.
10/20/97 *New Orleans Times-Picayune*

It's not Danny's fault. It's not Health's fault. It's our fault as an offense on what we're doing right now. Coaches, players—it's all out fault. 10/20/97 New Orleans Times-Picayune

About Danny Wuerffel:

You saw the game. He got beat up. I was surprised he was able to stand up at the end of the game. They practically tore his arm out of the socket. 10/20/97 *New Orleans Times-Picayune*

Midseason Assessment

The season is half over. We're 2-6. We've got a woeful record. We've looked terrible on offense. Our defense evidently has played pretty well to be where it's rated. If we can correct some things on offense, we will be a better team. But until we do, they are only words.
10/24/97 New Orleans Times-Picayune

All you have to do is look at the roster. There is not many places to go. We've tried everybody. We have done everything there is to do. 10/20/97 *New Orleans Times-Picayune*

On Saints players:

Maybe their ultimate desire is not to be with this organization. That's fine. Whether you want to be here next year or you want to be somewhere else, it's still important that you do your job this year. We have an obligation to the guy upstairs who signs the checks [owner Tom Benson]. Right now, we're not fulfilling that obligation. We have a long way to go before we really honor what we're supposed to be doing as employees. 11/5/97 New Orleans Times-Picayune

I am not going to be reluctant to [change quarterbacks]. You've got to win. If somebody is not getting the job done, then maybe that is not their day. So bring somebody else in and see if we can get it done. 11/7/97 *New Orleans Times-Picayune*

I don't understand the game as well as I did when I left it. It's changed, and it's hard... It's hard to get the pulse of a football team here right now. I've gone through every speech I've ever given and every quote I've ever known and everything I've ever believed. I believe they hear it, and I believe they believe it. But I don't believe it makes that much an impact anymore. 11/10/97 New Orleans Times-Picayune

I've never been this tired at night in my life. It's not just a physical thing. I know it's not. It's a mental thing. I've never got as tired as I've got here in my life. 11/10/97 *New Orleans Times-Picayune*

49ERS 23, SAINTS 0

I don't know if you're ever going to catch San Francisco taking anybody for granted. But if they're going to take anybody for granted, we'd be the guys they take for granted. I guarantee you that. 10/25/97 New Orleans Times-Picayune

It doesn't matter [who starts]. What's the difference? Nothing matters. You think I'm kidding? It doesn't matter. Until we establish a running game and have people up front blocking, it doesn't matter who you play at quarterback. 10/27/97 New Orleans Times-Picayune

SAINTS 13, RAIDERS 10

I just like to beat the Raiders. This was a big game for [owner] Tom Benson. He wants to beat the Raiders bad. He has no love lost for the Raiders. A lot of people don't. [Raiders coach] Joe Bugel is a great friend, a great guy, but when you go out and you play one of the supposed premier organizations in football, that's where you've got to start. And you've got to start by beating them on their own terms—by playing tough, hard, aggressive football. 11/11/97 *New Orleans Times-Picayune*

Saints special teams coach Bobby April:
He was after everybody, including the officials. I have a book that I read to my kids. It's called 'The Big, Hungry Bear.' That was Mike today. 11/10/97 New Orleans Times-Picayune

Ditka on yanking Heath Shuler when he thought Shuler was ignoring him:
I just wanted him to say 'Hello' when he comes off the field. 11/10/97 *New Orleans Times-Picayune*

If they want to put a camera on me, fine. I mean, I've got to get a phone call from my mother wondering if I'm all right. I said, "Why

wouldn't I be all right?" She said, "Well, at times you didn't look all right." I said I didn't know what they showed. I really don't care. That's not important to me. 11/13/97 New Orleans Times-Picayune

SAINTS 20, SEAHAWKS 17 (OT)

I have to thank God; I really do. Because He's the only one who could have written that script. I've never seen anything like that in my life. I've never seen the turn of events where the ball went the way it went. I couldn't explain it. You couldn't explain it. It just happened. 11/17/97 *New Orleans Times-Picayune*

When asked why with a minute left in the Saints-Seahawks game Ditka pulled Shuler for Nussmeier:
I don't know. I just do those things. There's just not a whole lot of analytical things that go with anything I do anymore. I'm so spontaneous. I'm half berserk half the time I'm out there. It was just a gut feeling. 11/17/97 New Orleans Times-Picayune

FALCONS 20, SAINTS 3

Saints quarterback Doug Nussmeier:
I had high hopes. I was looking forward to playing well, it being my first start and everything. I didn't play well. I didn't throw well. That's why we lost. 11/24/97 *New Orleans Times-Picayune*

At the press conference after the Falcons loss:
This team did not quit today. There is just not very much talent on offense. That's my fault. I picked them.. I have failed this football team by playing the way we played today. I'm embarrassed by it more for them than for me. I've been embarrassed in my life before. 11/24/97 New Orleans Times-Picayune

I don't have it anymore. Maybe the game has passed me by. Maybe all the experts were right. 11/24/97 *New Orleans Times-Picayune*

Saints defensive end Darren Mickell:
That's his decision. If you don't want to be here, it won't affect me. You want somebody who wants to be here and who is going to go

through the bad times with you. I didn't think he was serious.
11/25/97 New Orleans Times-Picayune

Saints fullback Ray Zellars:
Mike is frustrated like everyone else. Mike is not a quitter.
11/24/97 *New Orleans Times-Picayune*

**Ditka's comments following an
outburst during the Atlanta game:**
*I didn't do my job in the second half yesterday [at Atlanta]. I can't
control everything that happens on the field. I know this, and I learned
this a long time ago. But yet, I think I can. I think that I can will
things to happen, and I can't. I need to be with these guys, and make
these guys believe that we have as much a right to win as anybody
else in this league. That's what I want them to believe. That's what
I want to have happen here. That's all I care about. That's my only
goal. What I did yesterday I did in the heat of anger, disappointment
and everything else. And it was stupid; it was stupid.*
11/25/97 New Orleans Times-Picayune

A final thought for the New Orleans media:
I regret what I did say. But if I wouldn't have said it, there would be
no news in this town all last night. Let's face it. Let's be honest.
11/26/97 *New Orleans Times-Picayune*

You'll have to run me out of town first [before quitting].
11/27/97 New Orleans Times-Picayune

SAINTS 16, PANTHERS 13

We talked about being a team a couple of weeks ago and the players
remembered that, and I kind of forgot it last week. But they are a
team; maybe not a great team or a good team. But they are playing
hard as a team, and it's fun to watch. The sideline was fun to be on
today. 12/1/97 *New Orleans Times-Picayune*

Billy Joe [Hobert] did a great job... He made things happen.
12/1/97 New Orleans Times-Picayune

I know we're not all we're supposed to be. But these guys haven't quit trying. I think you can go somewhere with these guys. I think we're going in the right direction, contrary to what everybody else thinks. Carolina was a playoff team last year. They beat Dallas in the playoffs. To come here and beat them is a big win for us. I guess they got the best record of any team that we beat, so it must be the best win we've had. 12/1/97 *New Orleans Times-Picayune*

RAMS 34, SAINTS 27

Isaac Bruce looked awfully good. If he's that good, I'm glad we only play him twice a year. We didn't match up very well with Isaac Bruce. 12/13/97 New Orleans Times-Picayune

Saints quarterback Billy Joe Hobert:
In this game you always learn. I felt I was making some good decisions out there until that last interception. I didn't hold up my end. You can't keep putting your defense in holes like we did, expecting it to keep bending and not break. I don't care how good you are. You can't hold up game after game and win it for the team. The offense has to do it's part. 12/8/97 *New Orleans Times-Picayune*

Matter of fact, I'm not unhappy with the game, except for the score. 12/8/97 New Orleans Times-Picayune

Saints offensive coordinator Danny Abramowicz on the loss:
It was my fault, period. That's it. There's no real answer to it. I ran some play-action passes, and I thought it was going, so I stayed with that. And I stayed with it too long. Then one thing led to another, and I never got back into the running game. I don't know why I didn't do that. I'm aggravated at myself.
12/9/97 *New Orleans Times-Picayune*

SAINTS 27, CARDINALS 10

If you ask me what I liked about the game, I'll tell you how stupid I am. I liked the last four minutes when we got down face-to-face with them and ran the football. If you can do that and you can take some

time off the clock, then you deserve to win a game once in a while. We've got to get down in the foxhole with people and outslug them once in a while. 12/15/97 New Orleans Times-Picayune

This has been a long year for everybody—the players, you guys [media], the fans. Maybe we can finish this thing on a high note and let everybody have a merry Christmas.
12/15/97 *New Orleans Times-Picayune*

CHIEFS 25, SAINTS 13

We took the football against Kansas City, the best record in football, right down the field in the first quarter. We didn't score because we didn't execute on the last play. The receiver was open. The quarterback [Billy Joe Hobert] made a mistake. Everybody is entitled to a mistake. 12/28/97 New Orleans Times-Picayune

I'm proud of our guys. I love these guys. I want to coach them and I guarantee we will turn this around... We'll turn it around, and I'll say that in front of everybody. I've never said it, but I'll say it. These guys will fight. We made some mistakes out there, and our special teams hurt us, but we will be OK.
12/22/97 *New Orleans Times-Picayune*

Post Season Evaluation

I thought we'd be on our way to the Super Bowl right now, but it didn't happen. I thought there would be tickertape parades here, all over the country, hailing the Saints. My goodness, it didn't happen, that way. That doesn't mean it won't.
12/14/97 New Orleans Times-Picayune

There were a number of games that we could have won. If you try to explain to somebody, "Comprehend this: This team turned the ball over more than 50 times in a season and still won six games." That speaks to the way our defense and special teams must have played, because we certainly didn't do it on offense.
12/28/97 *New Orleans Times-Picayune*

We were in some very winnable games early in the year. But we didn't do it. Now, I'm not sitting here saying we're better than the 49ers or we're as good as the 49ers. But I am saying that we have to find a way to be as good or better if we're going to get where we want to go. 12/16/97 New Orleans Times-Picayune

When you take something over, even when you think you can get into people's minds and know how they think, you really can't. I think as this season went on, I got a feel more and more for the guys on our football team. I really believe they brought into what we were trying to do. They tried hard and worked hard at it. I think the majority of people really enjoyed what we tried to do, and they understand we were fair to them. I think they understand how far we've got to go and yet how close we are. We're not that far away. 12/28/97 *New Orleans Times-Picayune*

Getting Ready For 1998

On the 1997 draft:
I can honestly say, last year's draft wasn't my draft. It was the Saints' draft. It will always be the Saints' draft. These aren't Ditka's, Kuharich's, Lemmerman's or Franklin's. They are the Saints'. That's why it's important for us to do things as an organization.
12/28/97 New Orleans Times-Picayune

We're not going to have a shopping cart trying to fit a lot of things in there. We're just going to pick a couple of areas and probably target three players, if we decide that, then go after them. The main thing I'd like to do is make sure we do our own housework here first, find out what we can do about keeping the people we want here, here. Period. I'm not worried about bringing in other people. I think we have the players to win our division. That's our goal next year. 12/23/97 *New Orleans Times-Picayune*

If somebody else wants the first pick, fine. More power to them. But I don't want it. If you're saying I am seeking that [the No. 1 pick], or I would want that to draft a favorite player or a favorite son, I wouldn't

want to do that. Because I think it's unfair to the player, and it's unfair to us. If it happens, and we end up with the first pick, then we'll cross that road when we come to it.
11/6/97 New Orleans Times-Picayune

**Bill Kuharich responding to a reporters
question on Ditka's ability to evaluate talent:**
If you look back at his first season with the Bears, he did a similar thing. If you're going to judge Mike Ditka on evaluating talent, you're going to have to wait. It's layer upon layer upon layer. His first foundation or layer was he wanted a big man first. Coupled in that he wanted character, attitude, try-hard guys with talent. Guys who made plays in college. Guys who can get better from year to year. Once you lay that foundation, you come back the next year and you have the same approach, except this time you add play makers, That's where we're at for the second draft.
11/27/97 *New Orleans Times-Picayune*

I think we have to get an impact player—a receiver, running back, quarterback. Somebody who can make an impact our football team and make us better by the plays he can make.
12/28/97 New Orleans Times-Picayune

The Quarterback Situation in 1998

Honestly, I'd be very surprised if we went into camp next year with any more than those three guys. Maybe one more quarterback. But with those three guys I would be very surprised if they're not here. Very surprised. 11/7/97 *New Orleans Times-Picayune*

We've put some time and effort into Heath, and I don't think that's a wasted ticket at all. I think that's still a very live card. I really like Danny Wuerffel a lot...I think he can win in this league, and he can be a good football player. And, of course, I like Billy Joe a lot. I have nothing against Doug [Nussmeier] and nothing against Jake [Delhomme, who is on the Saints practice squad].
12/16/97 New Orleans Times-Picayune

SAINTS FREE AGENTS

Saints cornerback Eric Allen:
I'm willing to sit down and do anything I can to try and help this team out because I believe in this team, and I believe in the guys I'm playing with. If that means restructuring my contract...we'll sit down and talk about it. I want to be part of this team, because I think it's going to be successful. 12/13/97 *New Orleans Times-Picayune*

Saints wide receiver Randal Hill:
I do want to come back. I don't have a lot of say-so. But I want Mike Ditka to be the head coach. I want (Saints owner) Mr. Benson running the show and I want Billy Joe Hobert throwing the ball to me. 12/19/ 97 New Orleans Times-Picayune

Saints wide receiver Andre Hastings:
I'm not real concerned about the [contract] situation...definitely want to come back here, the way we've got things going. Our record doesn't show the improvement we've made. We're going in the right direction. I don't want to leave here and then we start winning and I'm not part of it. I've been through the bad part. I want to be here when we win and this city starts rocking.
12/19/97 *New Orleans Times-Picayune*

TOM BENSON ON DITKA'S FIRST SEASON

We all were sort of down as last year ended, and he gave us a spark we needed to feel good about ourselves and to revamp the whole organization. Mike is a presence, not only to the football players but to everybody. We need everybody in this club feeling good about this club, and working hard for one goal, and that is winning. Mike brings that. Now losing, I don't think there are two people in this world who hate losing more than Mike Ditka and Tom Benson. Both of us have to keep picking ourselves up by the seat of our pants after a loss. That's because Mike Ditka has always been a winner. Tom

Benson has always been a winner. This losing is for the berries.
We're not going to tolerate it. We're going to make changes. We're
not afraid of making changes. Some of them may not work out, but
at least we're going to try. Most of the fans appreciate that. Fans
don't like nothing to happen. This club now says, "We made an error,
and we're going to change." We got rid of players that Mike and
Bill Kuharich didn't want, and we're still paying for them. Bill
Kuharich and the others did an outstanding job so it would not affect
us a great deal as we go into '98 and '99.
12/21/97 New Orleans Times-Picayune

Mike Ditka is going to bring a winning ball club to New Orleans,
and we will be here until the job is done. I honestly feel that. Mike
is a very generous, very good person. He's a winner. As I look
around the National Football League, Mike Ditka is the right person
for the New Orleans Saints, and there's no doubt in my mind that he
will bring a winning club here.
12/21/97 *New Orleans Times-Picayune*

Success For the Saints in 1998 and 1999

When asked by a reporter if the Saints
could be a successful team by 1999:
Are you saying that a team that goes 6-10 [the Saints record in 1997]
can't go 12-4 the next year? If that's what you're saying, then that's
a fallacy, because it's happening all over the league. At Chicago we
went 3-6, then we went to 8-8 and we won five of the last six to get to
8-8. Then we went 10-6 and won Super Bowl XX at 15-1. The only
thing that I've ever said about the three years is that I think it's
important to be fair with the everybody. The moment that I feel that
I'm not wanted by the ownership, I wouldn't want to be here. To me,
that's important. Why would I tie up somebody's time and money if I
wasn't the guy? 12/28/97 New Orleans Times-Picayune

THE 1998 DRAFT

Following are the top five picks made by the New Orleans Saints in the 1998 draft:

Kyle Turley, OT, San Diego State
Cameron Cleeland, TE, Washington
Fred Weary, DB, University of Florida
Julian Pittman, DE, Florida State
Wilmont Perry, RB, Livingstone

EVALUATING THE DRAFT

I know that people can argue for picking skill positions, and I don't argue against it. Now whether we're right or wrong, we'll figure that out later. But I think you've got to look at what we're trying to do. We're trying to put some pieces in the puzzle that aren't there right now. We think we have some people in positions that will give us enough to do it at the running back position. And hopefully, we'll have some receivers emerge that will be a little better than people thought they would be. 4/19/98 New Orleans Times-Picayune

On Cameron Cleeland:
[Cleeland] brings something to the table that you don't find that often. This guy is the total package. 4/19/98 *New Orleans Times-Picayune*

On Kyle Turley:
I don't care if he's a surfer. We've got guys that ride motorcycles, and that's not very smart. We've got coaches who ride motorcycles, and that's not very smart. But he's a player. He's going to bring something to our football team that we need, and I talk about it a lot. It's toughness. He has skill, there's no question about it. He's a talent. He plays the game the way you'd like to see people play it at a young age. He gets after people. 4/19/98 New Orleans Times-Picayune